George Rainsford Fairbanks

The Spaniards in Florida

Comprising the notable settlement of the Huguenots in 1564, and the history and antiquities of St. Augustine, founded a.d. 1565

George Rainsford Fairbanks

The Spaniards in Florida
Comprising the notable settlement of the Huguenots in 1564, and the history and antiquities of St. Augustine, founded a.d. 1565

ISBN/EAN: 9783337289164

Printed in Europe, USA, Canada, Australia, Japan

Cover: Foto ©ninafisch / pixelio.de

More available books at **www.hansebooks.com**

THE SPANIARDS IN FLORIDA,

COMPRISING THE NOTABLE SETTLEMENT

OF THE

HUGUENOTS IN 1564,

AND THE

HISTORY AND ANTIQUITIES

OF

ST. AUGUSTINE,

FOUNDED A. D. 1565.

GEORGE R. FAIRBANKS,

VICE-PRESIDENT FLORIDA HISTORICAL SOCIETY; HONORARY MEMBER NEW-YORK HISTORICAL SOCIETY; LECTURER ON AMERICAN HISTORY IN THE UNIVERSITY OF THE SOUTH.

JACKSONVILLE, FLA.
COLUMBUS DREW.
1868.

RESPECTFULLY INSCRIBED

TO

BUCKINGHAM SMITH, ESQ.,
U. S. SECRETARY OF LEGATION AT MADRID,

TO WHOSE EFFORTS IN THE

DISCOVERY AND PRESERVATION OF THE HISTORY AND ANTIQUITIES OF THE SPANISH DOMINION IN AMERICA,

A GRATEFUL ACKNOWLEDGMENT

IS DUE FROM

AMERICAN SCHOLARS.

PREFACE.

This volume, relating to the history and antiquities of the oldest settlement in the United States, has grown out of a lecture delivered by the author, and which he was desired to embody in a more permanent form.

The large amount of interesting material in my possession, has made my work rather one of laborious condensation than expansion.

I have endeavored to preserve as fully as possible, the style and quaintness of the old writers from whom I have drawn, rather than to transform or embellish the narrative with the supposed graces of modern diction; and, as much of the work consisted in translations from foreign idioms, this peculiarly un-English style, if I may so call it, will be more noticeably observed. I have mainly sought to give it a permanent value, as founded on the most reliable ancient authorities; and thus, to the extent of the ground which it covers, to make it a valuable addition to the history of our country.

In that portion of the work devoted to the destruction of the Huguenot colony and the forces of Ribault, I have in the main followed the Spanish accounts, desiring to divest the narrative of all suspicion of prejudice or unfairness; *Barcia*, the principal authority, as is well known, professing the same faith as Menendez, and studiously endeavoring throughout his work, to exalt the character of the Adelantado.

I am under great obligations to my friend, BUCKINGHAM SMITH, ESQ., for repeated favors in the course of its preparation.

PREFACE TO THE SECOND EDITION.

The interest evinced in the publication of the first edition of this volume, in 1858, under the title of HISTORY AND ANTIQUITIES OF ST. AUGUSTINE, has induced the author to prepare a second edition for the press, under the present title, as being more exactly descriptive of that portion of the history of Florida embraced in its pages.

He hopes at no distant day to put to press the History of Florida, in a much more complete form, and embracing the chequered and various pictures of the many expeditions which sought either to found upon its shores a kingdom to satiate their ambition, or to find wealth commensurate with their desires.

A chapter of no mean interest in the history of Florida has been added since the first preface was written. Battles have been fought upon its soil, more considerable as to the numbers engaged and the fierceness of the fray, than any ever before recorded. But as this chapter forms a portion of the general history of the State rather than of the old city which played but an inconsiderable part in the contest, it does not fall within the purview of this work to make more than a brief mention of this period.

G. R. F.

University Place, Tenn.,
Oct. 1, 1868.

CONTENTS.

CHAPTER I.
Introductory 9

CHAPTER II.
First discovery, 1512 to 1565.—Juan Ponce de Leon 11

CHAPTER III.
Ribault, Laudonniere, and Menendez—Settlements of the Huguenots, and foundation of St. Augustine.—1562—1565—1568 13

CHAPTER IV.
The attack on Fort Caroline.—1565 19

CHAPTER V.
Escape of Laudonniere and others from Fort Caroline—Adventures of the fugitives 24

CHAPTER VI.
Site of Fort Caroline, afterwards called San Matteo 31

CHAPTER VII.
Menendez's return to St. Augustine—Shipwreck of Ribault—Massacre of part of his command.—A. D. 1565 38

CHAPTER VIII.
Fate of Ribault and his followers—Bloody massacre at Matanzas, 1565. 46

CHAPTER IX.
Fortifying of St. Augustine—Disaffections and mutinies—Approval of Menendez' acts by king of Spain.—1565—1568 54

CHAPTER X.
The notable revenge of Dominic de Gourgues—Return of Menendez—Indian Mission.—1568 60

CONTENTS.

CHAPTER XI.

Sir Francis Drake's attack upon St. Augustine—Establishment of missions—Massacre of missionaries at St. Augustine.—1586—1638..... 65

CHAPTER XII.

Subjection of the Apalachian Indians—Construction of the fort, sea wall, &c.—1638—1700.. 71

CHAPTER XIII.

Attack on St. Augustine by Gov. Moore of South Carolina—Difficulties with the Georgians.—1702—1732............................... 77

CHAPTER XIV.

Siege of St. Augustine by Oglethorpe.—1732—1740........................... 82

CHAPTER XV.

Completion of the castle—Descriptions of St. Augustine a century ago—English occupation of Florida.—1755—1763—1783............. 90

CHAPTER XVI.

Re-cession of Florida to Spain—Erection of the Parish Church—Change of flags.—1783—1821... 101

CHAPTER XVII.

Transfer of Florida to the United States—American occupation—Ancient buildings, &c.. 106

CHAPTER XVIII.

Present appearance of St. Augustine, as given by the author of Thanatopsis—Its climate and salubrity...................................... 110

CHAPTER XIX.

St. Augustine in its old age.—1565—1868................................. 118

THE HISTORY AND ANTIQUITIES

OF

ST. AUGUSTINE, Fla.

CHAPTER I.

INTRODUCTORY.

The Saint Augustine of the present and the St. Augustine of the past, are in striking contrast.

We see, to-day, a town less in population than hundreds of places of but few months' existence, dilapidated in its appearance, with the stillness of desolation hanging over it, its waters undisturbed except by the passing canoe of the fisherman, its streets unenlivened by busy traffic, and at mid-day it might be supposed to have sunk under the enchanter's wand into an almost eternal sleep.

With no participation in the active schemes of life, and no hopes for the future; with no emulation, and no feverish visions of future greatness; with no corner lots on sale or in demand; with no stocks, save those devoted to disturbers of the public peace; with no excitements and no events; a quiet, undisturbed, dreamy vision of still life surrounds its walls, and creates a sensation of entire repose, pleasant or otherwise, as it falls upon the heart of the weary wanderer sick of life's busy bustle, or upon the restless mind of him who looks to nothing as life except perpetual, unceasing action—the one rejoicing in its rest, the other chafing under its monotony. And yet, about the old city there clings a host of historic associations, that throw around it a charm which few can fail to feel.

Its life is in its past; and when we recall the fact that it was the first permanent settlement of the white man, by more than forty years, in this confederacy; that here for the first time, isolated within the shadows of the primeval forest, the civilization of the Old World made its abiding place, where all was new, and wild, and strange; that this now so insignificant place was the key of an empire; that upon its fate rested the destiny of a nation; that its occupation or retention decided the fate of a people; that it was itself a vice provincial court, boasted of its adelantados, men of the first mark and note, of its Royal Exchequer, its public functionaries, its brave men at arms; that its proud name, conferred by its monarch, *"Le siempre fiel Ciudad de San Augustin,"*—The ever faithful City of St. Augustine—stood out upon the face of history; that here the cross was first planted; that from the Papal throne itself rescripts were addressed to its governors; that the first great efforts at Christianizing the fierce tribes of America proceeded from this spot; that the martyr's blood was first here shed; that within these quiet walls the din of arms, the noise of battle, and the fierce cry of assaulting columns, have been heard;—Who will not then feel that we stand on historic ground, and that an interest attaches to the annals of this ancient city far more than is possessed by mere brick and mortar, rapid growth, or unwonted prosperity? Moss-grown and shattered, it appeals to our instinctive feelings of reverence for antiquity; and we feel desirous to know the history of its earlier days.

CHAPTER II.

' FIRST DISCOVERY, 1512 TO 1565—JUAN PONCE DE LEON.

AMONG the sturdy adventurers of the sixteenth century who sought both fame and fortune in the path of discovery, was Ponce de Leon, a companion of Columbus on his second voyage, a veteran and bold mariner, who, after a long and adventurous life, feeling the infirmities of age and the shadows of the decline of life hanging over him, willingly credited the tale that in this, the beautiful land of his imagination, there existed a fountain whose waters could restore youth to palsied age, and beauty to efface the marks of time.

The story ran that far to the north there existed a land abounding in gold and all manner of desirable things, but, above all, possessing a river and springs of so remarkable a virtue that their waters would confer immortal youth on whoever bathed in them; that upon a time a considerable expedition of the Indians of Cuba had departed northward in search of this beautiful country and these waters of immortality, who had never returned, and who, it was supposed, were in a renovated state, still enjoying the felicities of the happy land.

Furthermore, Peter Martyr affirms, in his second decade, addressed to the Pope, "that among the islands on the north side of Hispaniola, there is one about three hundred and twenty-five leagues distant, as they say which have searched the same, in the which is a continual spring of running water, of such marvelous virtue that the water thereof being drunk, perhaps with some diet, maketh old men young again. And here I must make protestation to your Holiness not to think this to be said lightly, or rashly; for they have so spread this rumor for a truth throughout all the court, that not only all the people, but also many of them whom wisdom or fortune have divided from the common sort, think it to be true." * Thoroughly believing in

---

* The fountain of youth is a very ancient fable; and the reader will be reminded of the amusing story of the accomplishment of this miracle, told in Hawthorne's Twice-Told Tales, and of the marvelous effects produced by imbibing this celebrated spring water.

the verity of this pleasant account, this gallant cavalier fitted out an expedition from Porto Rico, and in the progress of his search came upon the coast of Florida, on Easter Monday, 1512, supposing then, and for a long period afterwards, that it was an island. Partly in consequence of the bright spring verdure and flowery plains that met his eye, and the magnificence of the magnolia, the bay and the laurel, and partly in honor of the day, Pascua Florida, or Palm Sunday, and reminded, probably, of its appropriateness by the profusion of the cabbage palms near the point of his landing, he gave to the country the name of Florida.

On the 3d of April, 1512, three hundred and fifty-five years ago, he landed a few miles north of St. Augustine, and took possession of the country for the Spanish crown. He found the natives fierce and implacable; and after exploring the country for some distance around, and trying the virtue of all the streams, and growing neither younger nor handsomer, he left the country without making a permanent settlement.

The subsequent explorations of Narvaez, in 1526, and of De Soto, in 1539, were made in another portion of our State, and do not bear immediately upon the subject of our investigation, although forming a most interesting portion of our general history.

CHAPTER III.

RIBAULT, LAUDONNIERE, AND MENENDEZ—SETTLEMENTS OF THE HUGUENOTS, AND FOUNDATION OF ST. AUGUSTINE.

1562—1565—1568.

The settlement of Florida had its origin in the religious troubles experienced by the Huguenots under Charles IX. in France.

Their distinguished leader, Admiral Coligny, as early as 1555 projected colonies in America, and sent an expedition to Brazil, which proved unsuccessful. Having procured permission from Charles IX. to found a colony in Florida— a designation which embraced in rather an indefinite manner the whole country from the Chesapeake to the Tortugas— he sent an expedition in 1562 from France, under command of Jean Ribault, composed of many young men of good family. They first landed at the St. John's River, where they erected a monument, but finally established a settlement at Port Royal, South Carolina, and erected a fort. After some months, however, in consequence of dissensions among the officers of the garrison, and difficulties with the Indians, this settlement was abandoned.

In 1564 another expedition came out under the command of Réné de Laudonnière, and made their first landing at the River of Dolphins, being the present harbor of St. Augustine, and so named by them in consequence of the great number of Dolphins (Porpoises) seen by them at its mouth. They afterwards coasted to the north, and entered the River St. Johns, called by them the River May.

Upon an examination of this river, Laudonnière concluded to establish his colony on its banks; and proceeding about two leagues above its mouth, built a fort upon a pleasant hill of "mean height," which, in honor of his sovereign, he named Fort Caroline.

The colonists after a few months were reduced to great distress, and were about taking measures to abandon the country a second time, when Ribault arrived with reinforcements.

It is supposed that intelligence of these expeditions was communicated by the enemies of Coligny to the court of Spain.

Jealousy of the aggrandizement of the French in the New World, mortification for their own unsuccessful efforts in that quarter, and a still stronger motive of hatred to the faith of the Huguenot, induced the bigoted Philip II. of Spain, to dispatch Pedro Menendez de Aviles, a brave, bigoted and remorseless soldier, to drive out the French colony, and take possession of the country for himself.

The compact made between the King and Menendez was, that he should furnish one galleon completely equipped, and provisions for a force of six hundred men; that he should conquer and settle the country. He obligated himself to carry one hundred horses, two hundred horned cattle, four hundred hogs, four hundred sheep and some goats, and five hundred slaves, (for which he had a permission free of duties), the third part of which should be men, for his own service and that of those who went with him, to aid in cultivating the land and building. That he should take twelve priests, and four fathers of the Jesuit order. He was to build two or three towns of one hundred families, and in each town should build a fort according to the nature of the country. He was to have the title of Adelantado of the country, as also to be entitled a Marquis, and his heirs after him, to have a tract of land, receive a salary of 2,000 ducats, a percentage of the royal duties, and have the freedom of all the other ports of New Spain.*

His force consisted, at starting, of eleven sail of vessels, with two thousand and six hundred men; but, owing to storms and accidents, not more than one half arrived. He came upon the coast on the 28th August, 1565, shortly after the arrival of the fleet of Ribault. On the 7th day of September, Menendez cast anchor in the River of Dolphins, the harbor of St. Augustine. He had previously discovered and given chase to some of the vessels of Ribault, off the mouth of the River May. The Indian village of Selooe then stood upon the site of St. Augustine, and the landing of Menendez was upon the spot where the city of St. Augustine now stands.

Fray Francisco Lopez de Mendoza, the Chaplain of the Expedition, thus chronicles the disembarkation and attendant ceremonies:—

"On Saturday the 8th day of September, the day of the nativity

---

* Barcia Ensayo, Cron. 66.

of our Lady, the General disembarked, with numerous banners displayed, trumpets and other martial music resounding, and amid salvos of artillery.

"Carrying a cross, I proceeded at the head, chanting the hymn *Te Deum Laudamus*. The General marched straight up to the cross, together with all those who accompanied him; and, kneeling, they all kissed the cross. A great number of Indians looked upon these ceremonies, and imitated whatever they saw done. Thereupon the General took possession of the country in the name of his Majesty. All the officers then took an oath of allegiance to him, as their general, and as adelantado of the whole country."

The name of St. Augustine was given, in the usual manner of the early voyagers, because they had arrived upon the coast on the day dedicated in their calendar to that eminent saint of the primitive church, revered alike by the good of all ages for his learning and piety.

The first troops who landed, says Mendoza, were well received by the Indians, who gave them a large mansion belonging to the chief, situated near the banks of the river. The engineer officers immediately erected an entrenchment of earth, and a ditch around this house, with a slope made of earth and fascines, these being the only means of defense which the country presents; for, says the father with surprise, "there is not a stone to be found in the whole country." They landed eighty cannon from the ships, of which the lightest weighed two thousand five hundred pounds.

But in the mean time Menendez had by no means forgotten the errand upon which he principally came; and by inquiries of the Indians he soon learned the position of the French fort and the condition of its defenders. Impelled by necessity, Laudonnière had been forced to seize from the Indians food to supply his famished garrison, and had thus incurred their enmity, which was soon to produce its sad results.

The Spaniards numbered about six hundred combatants, and the French about the same; but arrangements had been made for further accessions to the Spanish force, to be drawn from St. Domingo and Havana, and these were daily expected.

It was the habit of those days to devolve almost every event upon the ordering of a special providence; and each nation had come to look upon itself almost in the light of a peculiar people, led like the Israelites of old by signs and wonders; and as in their own view all their actions were directed by the design of advancing God's glory as well as their own purposes, so the blessing of Heaven would surely accompany them in all their undertakings.

So believed the Crusaders on the plains of Palestine; so believed the conquerors of Mexico and Peru; so believed the Puritan settlers of New England (alike in their Indian wars and their oppressive social polity); and so believed, also, the followers of Menendez and of Ribault; and in this simple and trusting faith, the worthy chaplain gives us the following account of the miraculous escape and deliverance of a portion of the Spanish fleet:—

"God and his Holy Mother have performed another great miracle in our favor. The day following the landing of the General in the fort, he said to us that he was very uneasy because his galley and another vessel were at anchor, isolated and a league at sea, being unable to enter the port on account of the shallowness of the water; and that he feared that the French might come and capture or maltreat them. As soon as this idea came to him he departed, with fifty men, to go on board of his galleon. He gave orders to three shallops which were moored in the river to go out and take on board the provisions and troops which were on board the galleon. The next day, a shallop having gone out thither, they took on board as much of the provisions as they could, and more than a hundred men who were in the vessel, and returned towards the shore; but half a league before arriving at the bar they were overtaken by so complete a calm that they were unable to proceed further, and thereupon cast anchor and passed the night in that place. The day following at break of day they raised anchor as ordered by the pilot, as the rising of the tide began to be felt. When it was fully light they saw astern of them at the poop of the vessel, two French ships which during the night had been in search of them. The enemy arrived with the intention of making an attack upon us. The French made all haste in their movements, for we had no arms on board, and had only embarked the provisions. When day appeared, and our people discovered the French, they addressed their prayers to our Lady of *Bon Secours d'Utrera*, and supplicated her to grant them a little wind, for the French were already close up to them. They say that *Our Lady* descended, herself, upon the vessel; for the wind freshened and blew fair for the bar, so that the shallop could enter it. The French followed it; but as the bar has but little depth and their vessels were large, they were not able to go over it, so that our men and the provisions made a safe harbor. When it became still clearer they perceived besides the two vessels of the enemy, four others at a distance, being the same which we had seen in port the evening of our arrival. They were well furnished with both troops and artillery, and had directed themselves for our galleon and the other ship, which were alone at sea. In this circumstance God accorded us two favors. The first was, that the same evening after they had discharged the provisions and the troops I have spoken of, at midnight the galleon and other vessel put to sea without being perceived by the enemy;

the one for Spain, and the other for Havana, for the purpose of seeking the fleet which was there; and in this way neither was taken.

"The second favor, by which God rendered us a still greater service, was that on the day following the one I have described there arose a storm, and so great a tempest that certainly the greater part of the French vessels must have been lost at sea; for they were overtaken upon the most dangerous coast I have ever seen, and were very close to the shore; and if our vessels, that is, the galleon and its consort, are not shipwrecked, it is because they were already more than twelve leagues off the coast, which gave them the facility of running before the wind, and maneuvering as well as they could, relying upon the aid of God to preserve them."*

Menendez had ascertained from the Indians that a large number of the French troops had embarked on board of the vessels which he had seen off the harbor, and he had good ground for believing that these vessels would either be cast helpless upon the shore, or be driven off by the tempest to such a distance as would render their return for some days impossible. He at once conceived the project of attacking the French fort upon the river May, by land.

A council of war was held, and after some discussion, for the most part adverse to the plan proposed by him, Menendez spoke as follows:

"Gentlemen and Brothers! we have before us now an opportunity which if improved by us will have a happy result. I am satisfied that the French fleet which four days since fled from me, and has now come to seek me, has been reinforced with the larger part of the garrison of their fort, to which, nor to port, will they be able to return for many days according to appearances; and since they are all Lutherans, as we learned before we sailed from Spain, by the edicts which Jean Ribault published before embarking, in order that no Catholic at the peril of his life should go in his fleet, nor any Catholic books be taken; and this they themselves declared to us the night they fled from us, and hence our war must be to blood and fire, not only on account of the orders we are under, but because they have sought us in order to destroy us, that we should not plant our holy religion in these regions, and to establish their own abominable and crazy sect among the Indians; so that the more promptly we shall punish them, we shall the

---

* The galleon spoken of was Menendez's own flag ship, the El Pelayo, the largest vessel in his fleet, fitted out at his own expense, and which had brought four hundred men. He had put on board of her a lieutenant and some soldiers, besides fifteen Lutherans as prisoners, whom he was sending home to the Inquisition at Seville. The orders to his officers were to go as speedily as possible to the island of Hispaniola, to bring provisions and additional forces. Upon the passage, the Lutheran prisoners, with some Levantine sailors, rose upon the Spaniards, killed the commander, and carried the vessel into Denmark. Menendez was much chagrined when he ascertained the fate of his favorite galleon, a long period afterwards.

more speedily do a service to our God and our king, and comply with our conscience and our duty.

"To accomplish this, we must choose five hundred arquebuse men and pikemen, and carry provisions in our knapsacks for eight days, divided into ten companies, each one with its standard and its captain, and go with this force by land to examine the settlements and fort of our enemies; and as no one knows the road, I will guide you within two points by a mariner's compass; and where we cannot get along, we will open a way with our axes; and moreover, I have with me a Frenchman who has been more than a year at their fort, and who says he knows the ground for two leagues around the fort.

"If we shall arrive without discovery, it may be that falling upon it at daylight we may take it, by planting upon it twenty scaling ladders, at the cost of fifty lives. If we are discovered, we can form in the shelter of the wood, which I am assured is not more than a quarter of a league distant, and planting there ten standards, send forward a trumpeter requiring them to leave the fort and the country, and return to their own country, offering them ships and provisions for the voyage. They will imagine that we have a much greater army with us, and they may surrender; and if they do not, we shall at least accomplish that they will leave us undisturbed in this our own settlement, and we shall know the way, so that we may return to destroy them the succeeding spring."

After some discussion it was concluded that after hearing mass they should undertake the expedition on the third day. Considerable opposition was manifested on the part of the officers; but, with a consummate knowledge of human nature, the Adelantado got up the most splendid dinner in his power, and invited his recreant officers to the repast, and dexterously appealed to their fears, as well as their pride, and overcame their reluctance to undertake the unknown dangers of a first march through Florida at a wetseason, an actual acquaintance with which would still more have dampened their ardor.

The troops assembled promptly upon the day appointed, at the sound of the trumpet, the fife and the drum, and they all went to hear mass, except Juan de Vicente, who said he had a disorder of the stomach, and in his leg; and when some friends wished to urge his coming, he replied: "I vow to God, that I will wait until the news comes that our force is entirely cut off, when we who remain will embark in our three vessels, and go to the Indies, where there will be no necessity of our all perishing like beasts."

This Juan Vicente seems to have been an apt specimen of a class of croakers not peculiar to any age or country. Of his future history the chronicle gives other instances of a similar spirit; and his sole claim to immortality, like that of many an other, is founded upon his impudence.

CHAPTER IV.

THE ATTACK ON FORT CAROLINE—1565.

The troops, having heard mass, marched out in order, preceded by twenty Biscayans and Asturians having as their captain Martin de Ochoa, a leader of great fidelity and bravery, furnished with axes to open a road where they could not get along. At this moment there arrived two Indians, who said that they had been at the fort six days before, and who "seemed like angels" to the soldiers, sent to guide their march. Halting for refreshment and rest wherever suitable places could be found, and the Adelantado always with the vanguard, in four days they reached the vicinity of the fort, and came up within less than a quarter of a league of it, concealed by a grove of pine trees. It rained heavily, and a severe storm prevailed. The place where they had halted was a very bad one, and very marshy; but he decided to stop there, and went back to seek the rearguard, lest they might lose the way.

About ten at night the last of the troops arrived, very wet indeed, for there had been much rain during the four days; they had passed marshes with the water rising to their waists, and every night there was so great a flood that they were in great danger of losing their powder, their matchfire, and their biscuit; and they became desperate, cursing those who had brought them there, and themselves for coming.

Menendez pretended not to hear their complaints, not daring to call a council as to proceeding or returning, for both officers and soldiers went forward very inquietly. Remaining firm in his own resolve, two hours before dawn he called together the Master of the Camp and the Captains to whom he said that during the whole night he had sought of God and his most Holy Mother that they would favor him and instruct him what he should do most advantageous for their holy service; and he was persuaded that they had all done the same. "But now, Gentlemen," he proceeded, "we must make some determination, finding ourselves exhausted, lost, without ammunition or provisions, and without the hope of relief."

Some answered very promptly, "Why should they waste their time in giving reasons? for, unless they returned quickly to St. Augustine, they would be reduced to eating palmettos;* and the longer they delayed, the greater trouble they would have."

The Adelantado said to them that what they said seemed very reasonable, but he would ask of them to hear some reasons to the contrary, without being offended. He then proceeded—after having smoothed down their somewhat ruffled dispositions, considerably disturbed by their first experience in encountering the hardships of such a march—to show them that the danger of retreat was then greater than an advance would be, as they would lose alike the respect of their friends and foes. That if, on the contrary, they attacked the fort, whether they succeeded in taking it or not, they would gain honor and reputation.

Stimulated by the speech of their General, they demanded to be led to the attack, and the arrangements for the assault were at once made. Their French prisoner was placed in the advance; but the darkness of the night and the severity of the storm rendered it impossible to proceed, and they halted in a marsh, with the water up to their knees, to await daylight.

At dawn the Frenchman recognized the country, and the place were they were, and where stood the fort; upon which the Adelantado ordered them to march, enjoining upon all, at the peril of their lives, to follow him; and coming to a small hill, the Frenchman said that behind that stood the fort, about three bow-shots distant, but lower down, near the river. The General put the Frenchman into the custody of Castaneda. He went up a little higher, and saw the river and one of the houses, but he was not able to discover the fort, although it was adjoining them; and he returned to Castaneda, with whom now stood the Master of the Camp and Ochoa, and said to them that he wished to go lower down, near to the houses which stood behind the hill, to see the fortress and the garrison, for, as the sun was now up, they could not attack the fort without a reconnoisance. This the Master of the Camp would not permit him to do, saying this duty appertained to him; and he went alone with Ochoa near to the houses, from whence they discovered the fort; and returning with their information, they came to

---

* A low palm, bearing an oily berry.

two paths, and leaving the one by which they came, they took the other. The Master of the Camp discovered his error, coming to a fallen tree, and turned his face to inform Ochoa, who was following him; and as they turned to seek the right path, he stopped in advance, and the sentinel discovered them, who imagined them to be French; but examining them he perceived they were unknown to him. He hailed, "Who goes there?" Ochoa answered, "Frenchmen." The sentinel was confirmed in his supposition that they were his own people, and approached them; Ochoa did the same; but seeing they were not French, the sentinel retreated. Ochoa closed with him, and with his drawn sword gave him a cut over the head, but did not hurt him much, as the sentinel fended off the blow with his sword; and the Master of the Camp coming up at this moment, gave him a thrust, from which he fell backwards, making a loud outcry. The Master of the Camp, putting his sword to his breast, threatened him with instant death unless he kept silence. They tied him thereupon, and took him to the General, who, hearing the noise, thought the Master of the Camp was being killed, and meeting with the Sergeant-major, Francisco de Recalde, Diego de Maya, and Andres Lopez Patino, with their standards and soldiers, without being able to restrain himself, he cried out, "Santiago! Upon them! Help of God, Victory! The French are destroyed. The Master of the Camp is in their fort, and has taken it." Upon which, all rushed forward in the path without order, the General remaining behind, repeating what he had said many times: himself believing it to be certain that the Master of the Camp had taken with him a considerable force, and had captured the fort.

So great was the joy of the soldiers, and such their speed, that they soon came up with the Master of the Camp and Ochoa, who was hastening to receive the reward of carrying the good news to the General of the capture of the sentinel. But the Master of the Camp, seeing the spirit which animated the soldiers, killed the sentinel, and cried out with a loud voice to those who were pressing forward, "Comrades! do as I do. God is with us;" and turned, running towards the fort, and meeting two Frenchmen on the way, he killed one of them, and Andres Lopez Patino the other. Those in the environs of the fort, seeing this tragedy enacted, set up loud outcries; and in order to know the cause of the alarm, one of the Frenchmen within opened the postern of the principal gate, which he had no sooner done than it was observed by the Master of the Camp; and throwing himself upon him, he killed him, and entered the gate, followed by the most active of his followers.

The French, awakened by the clamor, some dressed, others in their night-clothes, rushed to the doors of their houses to see what had happened; but they were all killed, except sixty of the more wary, who escaped by leaping the walls.

Immediately the standards of the Sergeant-major and of Diego Mayo were brought in, and set up by Rodrigo Troche and Pedro Valdes Herrera, with two cavaliers, at the same moment. These being hoisted, the trumpets proclaimed the victory, and the bands of soldiers who had entered opened the gates and sought the quarters, leaving no Frenchman alive.

The Adelantado hearing the cries, left Castaneda in his place to collect the people who had not come up, who were at least half the force, and went himself to see if they were in any danger. He arrived at the fort running; and as he perceived that the soldiers gave no quarter to any of the French, he shouted, "That at the penalty of their lives they should neither wound nor kill any woman, cripple, or child under fifteen years of age." By which seventy persons were saved; *the rest were all killed!*

Renato de Laudonnière, the Commander of the fort, escaped with his servant and some twenty or thirty others, to a vessel lying in the river.

Such is the Spanish chronicle, contained in Barcia, of the capture of Fort Caroline. Its details in the main correspond with the account of Laudonnière, and of Nicolas Challeux, the author of the letter printed at Lyons, in France, under date of August, 1566, by Jean Saugrain. In some important particulars, however, the historians disagree. It has been already seen that Menendez is represented as having given orders to spare all the women, maimed persons, and all children under fifteen years of age. The French relations of the event, on the contrary, allege that an indiscriminate slaughter took place, and that all were massacred without respect to age, sex, or condition; but as this statement is principally made upon the authority of a terrified and flying soldier, it is alike due to the probabilities of the case, and more agreeable to the hopes of humanity, to lessen somewhat the horrors of a scene which has need of all the palliation that can be drawn from the slightest evidences of compassion on the part of that stern and bigoted leader.

The Spanish statement is further confirmed by other writers, who speak of a vessel being dispatched by Menendez subsequently to carry the survivors to Spain.

CHAPTER V.

ESCAPE OF LAUDONNIERE AND OTHERS FROM FORT CAROLINE.
ADVENTURES OF THE FUGITIVES.

The narratives of this event are found singularly full, there being no less than three accounts by fugitives from the massacre. The most complete of these is that of Nicolas de Challeux, a native of Dieppe, which was published in the following year. I have largely transcribed from this quaint and curious narrative, not only an account of the fullness of the details, but also for the light it throws upon the habits of thought and modes of expression of that day, when so much was exhibited of an external religious faith, and so many were found who would fight for their faith when they refused to adhere to its requirements. There are apparent, also, a close study of the Scriptures, a great familiarity with its language, a frequent use of its illustrations, and a disposition to attribute all things, with a reverent piety, to the direct personal supervision of the Almighty. By the aid of a map of the St. John's River, it will not be difficult to trace the perilous route of escape pursued by De Challeux and his companions, over obstacles much magnified by the terror of the moment and want of familiarity with the country:—

"The number of persons in the fort was two hundred and forty, partly of those who had not recovered from sea-sickness, partly of artisans and of women and children left to the care and diligence of Captain Laudonniere, who had no expectation that it was possible that any force could approach by land to attack him. On which account the guards had withdrawn for the purpose of refreshing themselves a little before sunrise, on account of the bad weather which had continued during the whole night, most of our people being at the time in their beds sleeping. The wicket gate open, the Spanish force, having traversed forests, swamps, and rivers, arrived at break of day, Friday, the 20th September, the weather very stormy, and entered the fort without any resistance, and made a horrible satisfaction of the rage and hate they had conceived against our nation. It was then who should best kill the most men, sick and well, women and little children, in such a manner that it is impossible to conceive of a massacre which could equal this for its barbarity and cruelty.

"Some of the more active of our people, jumping from their beds, slipped out and escaped to the vessel in the river. I was myself surprised, going to my duty with my clasp-knife in my hand; for upon leaving my cabin, I met the enemy, and saw no other means of escape but turning my back, and making the utmost possible haste to lead over the palisades, for I was closely pursued, step by step, by a pikeman and one with a partisan; and I do not know how it was, unless by the grace of God, that my strength was redoubled, old man as I am and grey-headed, a thing which at any other time I could not have done, for the rampart was raised eight or nine feet; I then hastened to secrete myself in the woods, and when I was sufficiently near the edge of the wood at the distance of a good bow-shot, I turned towards the fort and rested a little time, finding myself not pursued; and as from this place all the fort, even the inner-court was distinctly visible to me, looking there I saw a horrible butchery of our men taking place, and three standards of our enemies planted upon the ramparts. Having then lost all hope of seeing our men rally, I resigned all my senses to the Lord. Recommending myself to his mercy, grace and favor, I threw myself into the wood, for it seemed to me that I could find no greater cruelty among the savage beast, than that of our enemy which I had seen shown towards our people. But the misery and anguish in which I found myself then, straitened and oppressed, seeing no longer any means of safety upon the earth, unless by a special grace of our Lord, transcending any expectation of man, caused me to utter groans and sobs, and with a voice broken by distress to thus cry to the Lord:

"'O God of our fathers and Lord of all mercy! who hast commanded us to call upon Thee even from the depths of hell and the shades of death, promising forthwith thy aid and succor! show me, for the hope which I have in Thee, what course I ought to take to come to the termination of this miserable old age, plunged into the gulf of grief and bitterness; at least, cause that, feeling the effect of Thy mercy, and the confidence which I have conceived in my heart for Thy promises, they may not be snatched from me through fear of savage and furious wild beasts on one hand, and of our and Thy enemies on the other, who desire the more to injure us for the memory of Thy name which is invoked by us than for any other cause; aid me, my God! assist me, for I am so troubled that I can do nothing more.'

"And while I was making this prayer, traversing the wood, which was very thick and matted with briars and thorns, beneath the large trees where there was neither any road nor path, scarcely had I trailed my way half an hour, when I heard a noise like men weeping and groaning near me; and advancing in the name of God, and in the confidence of His succor, I discovered one of our people, named Sieur de la Blonderie, and a little behind him another, named Maitre Robert, well known to us all, because he had in charge the prayers at the fort.

"Immediately afterwards we found also the servant of Sieur d'Ully, the nephew of M. Lebreau, Master Jaques Trusse, and many others; and we assembled and talked over our troubles, and deliberated as to what course we could take to save our lives. One of our number, much esteemed as being very learned in the lessons of Holy Scripture, proposed after this manner: 'Brethren, we see to what extremity we are brought; in whatever direction we turn our eyes, we see only barbarism. The heavens, the earth, the sea, the forest, and men,—in brief, nothing favors us. How can we know that if we yield to the mercy of the Spaniards, they will spare us? and if they should kill us, it will be the suffering of but a moment; they are men, and it may be that, their fury appeased, they may receive us upon some terms; and, moreover, what can we do? Would it not be better to fall into the hands of men, than into the jaws of wild beasts, or die of hunger in a strange land?'

"After he had thus spoken, the greater part of our number were of his opinion, and praised his counsel. Notwithstanding, I pointed out the cruel animosity still unappeased of our enemies, and that it was not for any human cause of quarrel, that they had carried out with such fury their enterprise, but mainly (as would appear by the notice they had already given us) because we were of those who were reformed by the preaching of the Gospel; that we should be cowards to trust in men, rather than in God, who gives life to his own in the midst of death, and gives ordinarily his assistance when the hopes of men entirely fail.

"I also brought to their minds examples from Scripture, instancing Joseph, Daniel, Elias, and the other prophets, as well also the apostles, as St. Peter and St. Paul, who were all drawn out of much affliction, as would appear by means extraordinary and strange to the reason and judgment of men. His arm, said I, is not shortened, nor in any wise enfeebled; his power is always the same. Do you not recollect, said I the flight of the Israelites before Pharaoh? What hope had that people of escaping from the hands of that powerful tyrant? He had them, as it were, under his heel. Before them they had the sea, on either side inaccessible mountains.

"What then? He who opened the sea to make a path for his people, and made it afterwards to swallow up his enemies, can not he conduct us by the forest places of this strange country? While thus discoursing, six of the company followed out the first proposition, and abandoned us to go and yield themselves up to our enemies, hoping to find favor before them. But they learned, immediately and by experience, what folly it is to trust more in men than in the promise of the Lord. For having gone out of the wood, as they descended to the fort they were immediately seized by the Spaniards and treated in the same fashion as the others had been. They were at once killed and massacred, and then drawn to the banks of the river, where the others killed at the fort lay in heaps. We who remained in the wood continued to make our way, and drawing towards the sea, as well as we could judge, and as it pleased God to conduct our paths and to straiten our course, we soon arrived at the brow of a mountain and from there commenced to see the sea, but it was still at a great distance; and what was worse, the road we had to take showed itself wonderfully strange and difficult. In the first place, the mountain from which it was necessary for us to descend, was of such height and ruggedness, that it was not possible for a person descending to stand upright; and we should never have dared to descend it but for the hope we had of sustaining ourselves by the branches of the bushes, which were frequent upon the side of the mountain, and to save life, not sparing our hands which we had all gashed up and bloody, and even the legs and nearly all the body was torn. But descending from the mountain, we did not lose our view of the sea, on account of a small wood which was upon a little hill opposite to us; and in order to go to the wood it was requisite that we should traverse a large meadow, all mud and quagmire, covered with briars and other kind of strange plants; for the stalk was as hard as wood, and the leaves pricked our feet and our hands until the blood came, and being all the while in water up to the middle, which redoubled our pain and suffering. The rain came down upon us in such manner from heaven, that we were during all that time between two floods; and the further we advanced the deeper we found the water.

"And then thinking that the last period of our lives had come, we all embraced each other, and with a common impulse, we commenced to sigh and cry to the Lord, accusing our sins and recognizing the weight of his judgment upon us. 'Alas! Lord,' said we, 'what are we but poor worms of the earth? Our souls weakened by grief, surrender themselves into thy hands. Oh, Father of Mercy and God of Love, deliver us from this pain of death! or if thou wilt that in this desert we shall draw our last breath, assist us so that death, of all things the most terrible, shall have no advantage over us, but that we may remain firm and stable in the sense of thy favor and good-will, which we have too often experienced in the cause of thy Christ to give way to the spirit of Satan, the spirit of despair and of distrust; for if we die, we will protest now before thy Majesty, that we would die unto thee, and that if we live it may be to recount thy wonders in the midst of the assembly of thy servants.' Our prayers concluded, we marched with great difficulty straight towards the wood, when we came to a great river which ran in the midst of this meadow; the channel was sufficiently narrow but very deep, and ran with great force, as though all the field ran toward the sea. This was another addition to our anguish, for there was not one of our men who would dare to undertake to cross over by swimming. But in this confusion of our thoughts, as to what manner to pass over, I bethought myself of the wood which we had left behind us. After exhorting my comrades to patience and a continued trust in the Lord, I returned to the wood, and cut a long pole, with the good size clasp knife which remained in my hand from the hour the fort was taken; and I returned to the others, who awaited me in great perplexity. 'Now, then, comrades,' said I, 'let us see if God, by means of this stick, will not give us some help to accomplish our path.' Then we laid the pole upon the water, and each one by turn taking hold of the end of the pole, carried it by his side to the midst of the channel, when losing sight of him we pushed him with sufficient force to the other bank, where he drew himself out by the canes and other bushes growing along its borders; and by his example we passed over, one at a time; but it was not without great danger, and not without drinking a great deal of salt water, in such manner that our hearts were all trembling, and we were as much overcome as though we had been half drowned. After we had come to ourselves and had resumed courage, moving on all the time towards the wood, which we had remarked close to sea, the pole was not even needed to pass another creek, which gave us not much less trouble than the first; but by the grace of God, we passed it and entered the wood the same evening, where we passed the night in great fear and trembling, standing about against the trees.

"And, as much as we had labored, even had it been more, we felt no desire to sleep; for what repose could there be to spirits in such mortal affright? Near the break of day, we saw a great beast, like a deer, at fifty paces from us, who had a great head, eyes flaming, the ears hanging, and the higher parts elevated. It seemed to us monstrous, because of its gleaming eyes, wondrously large; but it did not come near us to do us any harm.

"The day having appeared, we went out of the wood and returned towards the sea, in which we hoped, after God, as the only means of saving our lives; but we were again cast down and troubled, for we saw before us a country of marsh and muddy quagmires, full of water and covered with briars, like that we had passed the previous day. We marched across this salt marsh; and, in the direction we had to take, we perceived among the briars a body of men, whom we at first thought to be enemies, who had gone there to cut us off; but upon close observation, they seemed in as sad a plight as ourselves, naked and terrified; and we immediately perceived that they were our own people. It was Captain Laudonniere, his servant-maid, Jacques Morgues of Dieppe (the artist), Francis Duval of Rouen, son of him of the iron crown of Rouen, Niguise de la Cratte, Nicholas the carpenter, the Trumpeter of Sieur Laudonniere, and others, who all together made the number of twenty-six men. Upon deliberating as to what we should do, two of our men mounted to the top of one of the tallest trees and discovered from thence one of our vessels, which was that of Captain Maillard, to whom they gave a signal, that he might know that we were in want of help. Thereupon he came towards us with his small vessel, but in order to reach the banks of the stream, it was necessary for us to traverse the briars and two other rivers similar to those which we passed the previous day; in order to accomplish which, the pole I had cut the day before was both useful and necessary, and two others which Sr. de Laudonniere had provided ; and we came pretty near to the vessel, but our hearts failed us from hunger and fatigue, and we should have remained where we were unless the sailors had given us a hand, which aid was very opportune; and they carried us, one after the other, to the vessel, on board of which we were all received well and kindly. They gave us bread and water, and we began afterwards, little by little, to recover our strength and vigor ; which was a strong reason that we should recognize the goodness of the Lord, who had saved us against all hope from an infinity of dangers and from death, by which we had been surrounded and assaulted from all quarters, to render him forevermore our thanks and praises. We thus passed the entire night recounting the wonders of the Lord, and consoled each other in the assurances of our safety.

"Daylight having come, Jacques Ribault, Captain of the Pearl, boarded us to confer with us respecting what was to done by us, and what means we should take for the safety of the rest of our men and the vessels. It was then objected, the small quanity of provisions which we had, our strength broken, our munitions and means of defense taken from us, the uncertainty as to the condition of our Admiral, and not knowing but that he had been shipwrecked on some coast a long distance from us, or driven to a distance by the tempest.

"We thereupon concluded that we could do no better than return to France, and were of the opinion that the company should divide into two parts, the one remaining on board the Pearl, the other under charge of Captain Maillard.

"On Friday, the twenty-fifth day of the month of September, we departed from this coast, favored by a strong northerly wind, having concluded to return to France, and after the first day our two ships were so far separated that we did not again encounter each other.

"We proceeded five hundred leagues prosperously, when, one morning about sunrise, we were attacked by a Spanish vessel, which we met as well as we could, and cannonaded them in such sort that we made them subject to our disposal, and battered them so that the blood was seen to overrun the scuppers. We held them then as surrendered and defeated; but there was no means of grappling her, on account of the roughness of the sea, for in grappling her there would be danger of our striking together, which might have sunk us; she also, satisfied with the affair, left us, joyful and thanking God that no one of us was wounded or killed in this skirmish except our cook.

"The rest of our passage was without any rencounter with enemies; but we were much troubled by contrary winds, which often threatened to cast us on the coast of Spain, which would have been the finishing touch to our misfortunes, and the thing of which we had the greatest horror. We also endured at sea many other things, such as cold and hunger; for be it understood that we, who escaped from the land of Florida, had nothing else for vestment or equipment, by day or by night, except our shirts alone, or some other little rag, which was a small matter of defence from the exposure to the weather; and what was more, the bread which we eat, and we eat it very sparingly, was all spoilt and rotten, as well also the water itself was all noisome, and of which, besides, we could only have for the whole day a single small glass.

"This bad food was the reason, on our landing, that many of us fell into divers maladies, which carried off many of the men of our company; and we arrived at last, after this perilous and lamentable voyage, at Rochelle; where we were received and treated very humanely and kindly by the inhabitants of the country and those of the city, giving us of their means, to the extent our necessities require; and assisted by their kindness we were each enabled to return to his own part of the country."*

Laudonnière's† narrative speaks more of his own personal escape; and that of Le Moyne‡ refers to this description of De Challeux, as containing a full and accurate account of what took place. Barcia mentions De Challeux, very contemptuously as a carpenter, who succeeding badly at his trade, took up that of preaching, but does not deny the truth of his narrative.

Those who separated from their comrades and threw themselves upon the enemies' mercy, are mentioned by the Spanish writers; but they are silent as to the treatment they received.

* Ternaux Compans.   † Hakluyt.   ‡ Brevis Narratio.

CHAPTER VI.

SITE OF FORT CAROLINE, AFTERWARDS CALLED SAN MATTEO.

It might naturally be supposed that a spot surrounded with so many thrilling and interesting associations, as the scene of the events we have just related, would have been commemorated either by tradition or by ancient remains attesting its situation. But, in truth, no recognized point now bears the appellation of Fort Caroline, and the antiquary can point at this day to no fosse or parapet, no crumbling bastion, no ancient helm or buckler, no shattered and corroded garniture of war mingled with the bones of the dead, as evidencing its position.

A writer who has himself done more to rescue from oblivion the historical romance of the South than any other,* has well said, "It will be an employment of curious interest, whenever the people of Florida shall happen upon the true site of the settlement and structure of Laudonnière, to trace out in detail these several localities, and fix them for the benefit of posterity. The work is scarcely beyond the hammer and chisel of some Old Mortality, who has learned to place his affections and fix his sympathies upon the achievements of the past."

With a consciousness of our unfitness to establish absolutely a memorial so interesting as the site of Fort Caroline must ever be, I shall endeavor to locate its position, upon the basis of reasons entirely satisfactory to myself, and measurably so, I trust, to others.

The account given by Laudonnière himself, the leader of the Huguenots, by whom Fort Caroline was constructed, is as follows:—After speaking of his arrival at the mouth of the river, which had been named the River May by Ribault, who had entered it on the first day of May, 1562, and had therefore given it that name, he says, "Departing from thence, I had not sailed three leagues up the river, still being followed by the Indians, crying still, 'amy,' 'amy,' that is to say, friend, but I discovered an hill of meane

---

*W. Gilmore Simms, Esq.

height, neare which I went on land, harde by the fieldes that were sowed with mil, at one corner whereof there was an house, built for their lodgings which keep and garde the mil. * * * * * * Now was I determined to searche out the qualities of the hill. Therefore I went right to the toppe thereof; where we found nothing else but cedars, palms, and bay trees of so sovereign odor that Balme smelleth not more sweetly. The trees were environed around about with vines bearing grapes, in such quantities that the number would suffice to make the place habitable. Besides the fertilitie of the soyle for vines, one may see mesquine wreathed about the trees in great quantities. Touching the pleasure of the place, the sea may be seen plain enough from it; and more than six great leagues off, towards the River Belle, a man may behold the meadows, divided asunder into isles and islet, enterlacing one another. Briefly, the place is so pleasent, that those which are melancholicke, would be inforced to change their humour. * *

"Our fort was built in form of a triangle; the side towards the west, which was towards the land, was inclosed with a little trench and raised with turf made in the form of a battlement, nine feet high; the other side, which was towards the river, was enclosed with a palisade of planks of timber, after the manner that Gabions are made; on the south line, there was a kind of bastion, within which I caused an house for the munition to be made. It was all builded with fagots and sand, saving about two or three foote high, with turfes whereof the battlements were made. In the middest, I caused a great court to be made of eighteen paces long, and the same in breadth. In the middest whereof, on the one side, drawing towards the south, I builded a corps de garde and an house on the other side towards the north. * * * * One of the sides that inclosed my court, which I made very faire and large, reached unto the grange of my munitions; and on the other side, towards the river, was mine own lodgings, round which were galleries all covered. The principal doore of my lodging was in the middest of the great place, and the other was towarde the river. A good distance from the fort I built an oven."

Jacob Le Moyne, or Jacques Morgues, as he is sometimes called, accompanied the expedition; and his *Brevis Narratio* contains two plates, representing the commencement of the construction of Fort Caroline, and its appearance when completed. The latter represents a much more finished fortification than could possibly have been constructed, but may be taken as a correct outline, I presume, of its general appearance.

Barcia, in his account of its capture, describes neither its shape nor appearance, but mentions the parapet nine feet high, and the munition house and store house.

From the account of Laudonnière and Le Moyne, it was situated near the river, on the slope or nearly at the foot of a hill.* Barcia speaks of its being behind a hill, and of descending towards it. The clerical-carpenter, Challeux, speaks of being able, after his escape, to look down from the hill he was on, into the court of the fort itself, and seeing the massacre of the French. As he was flying from the fort towards the sea, and along the river, and as the Spaniards came from a southeast direction, the fort must have been on the westerly side of a hill, near the river.

The distance is spoken of as less than three leagues by Laudonnière. Hawkins and Ribault say, the fort was not visible from the mouth of the river. It is also incidentally spoken of in Barcia as being two leagues from the bar. De Challeux, in the narrative of his escape, speaks of the distance as being about two leagues. In the account given of the expedition of De Gourgues, it is said to be, in general terms, about one or two leagues above the forts afterwards constructed on each side of the mouth of the river; and it is also mentioned in De Gourgues, that the fort was at the foot of a hill, near the water, and could be overlooked from the hill. The distance from the mouth of the river, and the nature of the ground where the fort was built, are thus made sufficiently definite to enable us to seek a location which shall fulfill both these conditions. It is hardly necessary to remark that there can be no question but that the fort was located on the south or easterly side of the river, as the Spaniards marched by land from St. Augustine in a northwesterly direction to Fort Caroline.

The River St. Johns is one of the largest rivers, in point of width, to be found in America, and is more like an arm of the sea than a river; from its mouth for a distance of fifteen miles, it is spread over extensive marshes, and there are few points where the channel touches the banks of the river. At its mouth it is comparatively narrow, but immediately extends itself over wide-spread marshes; and the first headland or shore which is washed by the channel is a place known as St. John's Bluff. Here the river runs

---

* Laudonnière says, "*joignant la montagne.*"

closely along the shore, making a bold, deep channel close up to the bank. The land rises abruptly on one side into a hill of moderate height, covered with a dense growth of pine, cedar, &c. This hill gently slopes to the banks of the river, and runs off to the southwest, where, at the distance of a quarter of a mile, a creek discharges itself into the river, at a place called "the Shipyard" from time immemorial.

I am not aware that any remains of Fort Caroline, or any old remains of a fortress, have ever been discovered here; but it must be recollected that this fort was constructed of sand and pine trees, and that three hundred years have passed away, with their storms and tempests, their rains and destructive influences—a period sufficent to have destroyed a work of much more durable character than sandy entrenchments and green pine stakes and timbers. Moreover, it is higly probable, judging from present appearances, that the constant abrasion of the banks still going on has long since worn away the narrow spot where stood Fort Caroline. It is also to be remarked, that as there is no other hill, or high land, or place where a fort could have been built, between St. John's Bluff and the mouth of the river, so it is also the fact that there is no point on the south side of the river where the channel touches high land, for a distance by water of eight or ten miles above St. John's Bluff.

The evidence in favor of the location of Fort Caroline at St. John's Bluff is, I think conclusive and irresistible, and accords in all points with the descriptions given as to distance, topography, and points of view.

It is within the memory of persons now living, that a considerable orange grove and somewhat extensive buildings, which existed at this place, then called San Vicente, have been washed into the river, leaving at this day no vestiges of their existence. It has been occupied as a Spanish fort within fifty years; yet so rapid has been the work of time and the elements, that no remains of such occupation are now to be seen.

The narratives all speak of the distance from the mouth of the river as about two leagues; and in speaking of so short a distance the probability of exactness is much greater than when dealing with longer distances.

As to the spot itself, it presents all the natural features mentioned by Laudonnière; and it requires but a small spice of enthusiasm and romance that it be recognized as a "goodlie and pleasante spotte," by those who might like the abundance of the wild grapes and the view of the distant salt meadows, with their "iles and islets, so pleasante that those which are melancholike would be inforced to change their humour."

It is but proper, however, to say, that at a plantation known as Newcastle there is a high range of ground, and upon this high ground the appearance of an old earth-workof quadrangular form; but this point is distant some six leagues from the mouth of the river, is flanked by a deep bay or marsh to the southeast, and the work is on the top of the hill and not at its foot, is quadrangular and not triangular, and is a considerable distance from the water. These earthworks, I am satisfied, are Spanish or English remains of a much later period.

By examining a map of the St. John's river, the first projecting land on the south side, lying east of the second township line marked from the coast, will be found nearly to indicate the point known as St. John's Bluff. On the eastern face the bluff is quite high and precipitous—being possibly the "brow of the mountain" mentioned by De Challeux—and immediately beyond is a deep indentation of the shore-line of several miles in circuit, within which is an immense tract of sea-marsh, interspersed with small islands, and cut up by narrow channels. Through this the fugitives may be supposed to have crossed, and, reaching the high lands which hem in the marsh near the mouth of the river, were enabled to view the vessels which offered them rescue. About the year 1856 a handful of small copper coins were accidentally found near the eastern margin of this marsh, in the rear of what is now known as Mayport Mill. Some few were at first found on the ground, as if accidentally exposed, and upon removing the earth for a slight depth the remainder were discovered. They were distributed among several gentlemen in Florida, and Mr. Buckingham Smith, at that time and more recently made the history of the coins a subject of especial inquiry in Spain.

Just before putting the second edition of this work to press, the following letter was received by the publisher of this volume, and is given as matter of interest in connection with the locality referred to:

MADRID, August 15, 1868.

MY DEAR SIR:—I brought with me from Florida, as I proposed, three copper coins of those found with others of the same sort many years ago, on the St. Johns river near the old site of Fort Caroline, in what the French three centuries ago called the Vale of Laudonniere,

that I might have them examined in Europe. There were none of the
sort in the British Museum, with which they might be compared, and
in the Bibliothique Imperial I could only learn that they were Spanish.
On my arrival here I gave them for inspection to Senor Bermudez, a
long time in charge of the national collection of such like antiquities,
second only in extent and value to that of Paris: and showed them
also to other of my friends learned in numismatics. The work of A.
Heiss, now making its appearance in numbers, with the title *Description General de las monedas Hispano—Christianas desde la invasion
de los Arabes*, has been also consulted, and this is the amount of all
the conclusions, the inscriptions on each coin being nearly the same:

† KAROLVS.ET.IOANNA RE.
Two II in the midst, with crowns upon them; to the right P, to the left S;
in the middle a square point.
REVERSO:
Same—same—same—REGIS.
A Y in the middle, crowned; to the right IIII; to the left F.

They were struck for Dona Juana and Carlos I., Empr. Charles V.,
between the years 1516 and 1555. The Y is supposed to refer to Ysa-
bel: the double I to Joanna I., or may be to the columns of Hercules,
and the crowns upon them to those of Castilla and Aragon. On later
silver coins, not so rude, the columns are placed with the words *plus
ultra*, as you may have observed on a Spanish dollar. The IIII (on
some 4,) means four maravedises, the value of which have varied: at
present 25 of these would be the value of a real. These coins are uncommon; in good preservation, very rare. The curiosity so many of
us have had for a number of years about these matters, I believe is at
last satisfied.

I have visited the town of Aviles, a league from the Bay of Biscay,
whence Pedro Menendez came, and brought his fleet to Florida, three
centuries ago. I saw his tomb, and not far off the chapel of the family
of one of his companions. There is no stranger any where to be heard
of in all that country; every thing is intensely and old Spanish in
every aspect. Going home late one evening, I was accosted by a native in good English. He said the town was rarely visited—three or
four Englishmen within his memory had passed through, and he supposed me to be the first person from the United States who had ever been
there. I told him I came from Florida, and, though rather late, was
returning the visit of Menendez to St. Augustine.

The estate of this old colonist is in the house of the Count of Ca-
nalejas, held by the Marquis of San Estevan, who is also by marriage
the Count of Revilla Gigedo. I called on him at his country seat in
Dania, and, detaining me to spend the day with him, gave orders to
have his family pictures and palace shown to me at Gijon, and his papers at a residence in Oviedo. Among the documents is a valuable one
for writing a life of Menendez. It is a draft for a letter in his own
hand, directed to his nephew, Governor of Florida, in which he ex-
presses his wish to be with him and away from business. He speaks
of the "invincible armada" which he had been appointed to com-

mand, and gives the number of his ships. This probably was the last thing he ever wrote, dated ten days before he died, as it is known that he died on the ninth day of his sickness. Of course I have a copy to show you.

Spain has greatly changed within the last eight years—impoverished itself, the people say, with improvements. The railroads traverse most parts, are well laid, durable, and the service good. The ancient monuments have begun to be cared for, are repaired, and in the charge of a commission of the government.

Give my best regards to friends about you, and believe me truly yours, BUCKINGHAM SMITH.

Mr. COLUMBUS DREW, Jacksonville, Fla.

CHAPTER VII.

MENENDEZ'S RETURN TO ST. AUGUSTINE—SHIPWRECK O RIBAULT—MASSACRE OF PART OF HIS COMMAND—

A. D. 1565.

AFTER an ineffectual attempt to induce those in the small vessels of the French to surrender, failing in this, the General concluded to return to St. Augustine, and send two of his vessels to the mouth of the river to intercept them.

Some of the fugitives from the fort fled to the Indians; and ten of these were given up to the Spaniards, to be butchered in cold blood, says the French account,—to be sent back to France, says the Spanish chronicle.

The 24th September being the day of St. Matthew, the name of the fort was changed to that of San Matheo, by which name it was always subsequently called by the Spaniards; and the name of St. Matthew was also given by them to the river, now called St. Johns, on which it is situated.

The Spaniards proceeded at once to strengthen the fortress, deepening and enlarging the ditch, and raised and strengthened the ramparts and walls in such manner, says the boastful Mendoza, "that if the half of all France had come to attack it, they could not have disturbed it;" a boast upon which the easy conquest of it by De Gourgues, three years subsequently, affords an amusing commentary. They also constructed, subsequently, two small forts at the mouth of the river, one on each side, which probably were located the one at Batten Island and the other at Mayport.

Leaving three hundred soldiers as a garrison under his son-in-law, De Valdez, Master of the Camp, who was now appointed Govenor of the fort, Menendez marched for St. Augustine, beginning now to feel considerable anxiety lest the French fleet, escaping from the tempest, might return and visit upon his own garrison at St. Augustine, the fate of Fort Caroline. He took with him upon his return but fifty soldiers, and, owing to the swollen waters, found great difficulty in retracing his route. When within a league of St. Augustine, he allowed one of the soldiers to go forward to announce his victory and safe return.

The garrison at St. Augustine had been in great anxiety respecting their leader, and from the accounts given by those who had deserted, they had feared the total loss of the expedition. The worthy Chaplain thus describes the return of Menendez :—

"The same day, being Monday, we saw a man coming, crying out loudly. I myself was the first to run to him for the news. He embraced me with transport, crying 'Victory! Victory! The French fort is ours.' I promised him the present which the bearer of good news deserves, and gave him the best in my power.

"At the hour of vespers our good General arrived, with fifty foot soldiers, very much fatigued. As soon as I learned that he was coming, I ran home and put on a new soutain, the best which I had, and a surplice, and going out with a crucifix in my hand, I went forward to receive him; and he, a gentleman and a good Christian, before entering kneeled and all his followers, and returned thanks to the Lord for the great favours which he had received. My companions and myself marched in front in procession, so that we all returned with the greatest demonstrations of joy."

When about to dispatch the two vessels in his harbor to the St. John's, to cut off the French vessels he had left there, he was informed that two sail had already been seen to pass the bar, supposed to contain the French fugitives.

Eight days after the capture of Fort Caroline, a fire broke out in the quarters of St. Augustine, which destroyed much treasure and provisions, and the origin of which was doubtful, whether to be ascribed to accident or design. Much dissatisfaction prevailed among the officers and soldiers, and the fire was looked upon with pleasure by some, as having a tendency to hasten their departure from a spot which offered few temptations or rewards, compared to Mexico or Peru.

On the very day of Menendez's return, a Frenchman was discovered by a fishing party on Anastasia Island, who, being taken, said he was one of a party of eighteen, sent in a small vessel, some days before, to reconnoitre the Spanish position; that they had been unable to keep the sea, and had been thrown ashore, about four leagues below, at the mouth of a river; that the Indians attacked and killed three of their number, and they thereupon escaped.

Menendez dispatched a captain and fifty men, to get off the vessel and capture any of the French who might be found. On their arrival at the place, they found that all the French had been killed by the Indians; but they succeeded in getting off the vessel. Menendez, feeling uneasy in reference to their encounter with the Indians, had followed on after the expedition, in company with the worthy Chaplain, to whom his promenade among the briars, vines, prickly cedars, chaparral, and prickly pears of Anastasia, seems to have been a true *via dolorosa*.

Upon their arrival, they found a considerable body of French upon the south side of an inlet, whose fires indicated their position.

The four vessels of Ribault, which had gone in pursuit of the Spaniards at St. Augustine, had been overtaken by the storm, and after keeping to sea with incredible effort, had been finally driven ashore upon the shoals of Canaveral,* with but little loss of life but a total loss of every thing else; they were thus thrown on shore without shelter from the elements, famished with hunger, borne down by disappointment, and utterly dispirited and demoralized. They were consumed, also, by the most painful uncertainty. Marching to the northward along shore, they discovered a skiff, and resolved to send a small number of persons in it, to make their way by sea to Fort Caroline, to bring succor to them from there. This boat succeeded in reaching the St. John's, where they were informed, by friendly Indians, of the fate which had befallen the fort; and subsequently they fell in with a Frenchman who had escaped, who related to them the whole disaster. Upon this they concluded to seek their own safety among the friendly Indians of St. Helena, rather than to be the useless bearers of the tidings of their misfortunes to their companions in arms.

There are several accounts of the sad fate which befel the followers of Ribault, the massacre of whom has been perpetuated by the memorial name given to its scene, "the bloody river of Matanzas," the ebb and flow of whose recurring tides for three hundred years have failed to wash out the record of blood which has associated this massacre of the Huguenots with the darkest scenes of earth's history. In consequence of the rank and number of the victims, the event produced various and somewhat contradictory accounts; but all stamped with a seal of reprobation and execration the act and the actors, without reference to creed or nationality. Challeux relates instances of cruel barbarity added to the atrocity of slaughter itself; and others, it appears, had given other versions, all in different degree pointing the finger of historic justice to mark and commemorate the crime against humanity.

---

* Canaveral, where Ribault was wrecked, must have been some point north of Mosquito Inlet, and not the cape now bearing that name, as he could not have crossed Mosquito Inlet in his march to Matanzas.

The Spanish historian, Barcia, aims to counteract this general condemnation, of which in his own language he says, "These calumnies, repeated in so many quarters, have sullied the fame of the Adelantado, being exaggerated by the heretics, and consented to by the Catholics, so that even the Father Felix Briot, in his annals, says that he caused them to be killed contrary to the faith which he had given them; which is altogether a falsehood, for the Adelantado did not give his word, nor would he when asked give it, to spare their lives, although they were willing to pay him for doing so; nor in the capture of Fort Caroline did he do more than has been related; and such is the account given by Doctor Salis de las Meras, brother-in-law to Donna Maria de Salis, wife of the Adelantado, who was present, and who, relating the punishment of the heretics, and the manner in which it was accomplished, says,—

"'The Adelantado occupied himself in fortifying his settlement at St. Augustine, as well as he could, to defend it from the French fleet if they should attack it. Upon the following day some Indians came and by signs informed them that four leagues distant there were a large number of Christians, who were unable to cross an arm of the sea or strait, which is a river upon the inner side of an inlet, which they were obliged to cross in order to come to St. Augustine. The Adelantado sent thither forty soldiers about dusk, and arrived about midnight near the inlet, where he commanded a halt until morning, and leaving his soldiers concealed, he ascended a tree to see what was the state of matters. He discovered many persons on the other side of the river, and their standards; and to prevent their passing over, he directed his men to exhibit themselves towards the shore, so that it might be supposed that he had with him a large force; and when they were discovered, a French soldier swam over, and said that the persons beyond the river were Frenchmen, that they had been wrecked in a storm, but had all saved their lives. The Adelantado asked what French they were? He answered, that they were two hundred of the people under command of Jean Ribault, Viceroy and Captain General of this country for the king of the French. He asked again, if they were Catholics or Lutherans? It was replied that they were all Lutherans, of the new religion; all of which was previously well known to the Adelantado, when he encountered their fleet with his vessels; and the women and children whom he had spared when he took their fort, had also so informed him; and he had found in the fort when he took it, six trunks filled with books, well bound and gilt; all of which were of the new sect, and from which they did not say mass, but preached their Lutheran doctrines every evening; all of which books he directed to be burnt, not sparing a single one.

"'The Adelantado then asked him why he had come over? He said he had been sent over by his Captain, to see what people they were. The General asked if he wished to return. He said, "Yes, but he desired to know what people they were." This man spoke very plainly, for he was a Gascon of San Juan de Suz. "Then tell him," said the Adelantado, "that it is the Viceroy and Captain General of this country for the king, Don Philip; and that his name is Pedro Menendez, and that he is here with some of his soldiery to ascertain what people those were, for he had been informed the day before that they were there, and the hour at which they came."

"'The French soldier went over with his message, and immediately returned, saying "that if they would pledge faith to his captain and to four other gentlemen, they would like to come and treat with him;" and they desired the loan of a boat, which the General had directed to bring some provisions to the river. The General instructed the messenger to say to his captain, "that he might come over securely under the pledge of his word," and then sent over for them the boat; and they crossed over. The Adelantado received them very well, with only ten of his followers; the others he directed to stay some distance off among some bushes, so that their number might appear to be greater than it was. One of the Frenchmen announced himself as captain of these people; and that in a great storm they had lost four galleons, and other vessels of the king of France, within a distance of twenty leagues of each other; and that these were the people from on board of one ship, and that they desired they would let them have a boat for this arm of the sea, and for another four leagues hence, which was at St. Augustine; that they desired to go to a fort which they held twenty leagues from there. It was the same fort which Menendez had taken. The Adelantado asked them "if they were Catholics or Lutherans?" He replied "that they were all of the New Religion." Then the Adelantado said to them, "Gentlemen, your fort is taken and its people destroyed, except the women, and children under fifteen years of age; and that you may be assured of this, among the soldiers who are here there are many things, and also there are here two Frenchmen whom I have brought with me, who said they were Catholics. Sit down here and eat, and I will send the two Frenchmen to you, as also the things which some of my soldiers have taken from the fort, in order that you may be satisfied.

"'The Adelantado having spoken thus, directed food to be given to them, and sent the two Frenchmen to them, and many things which the soldiers had brought from the fort, that they might see them, and then retired himself, to eat with his own people; and an hour afterwards, when he saw that the French had eaten, he went where they were and asked if they were satisfied of the truth of what he had told them. They said they were, and desired that for a consideration, he should give them vessels and ships' stores, that they might return to France. The Adelantado answered, "that he would do so with great pleasure if they were good Catholics, or if he had the ships for them; but he had not the vessels, having sent two to St. Matteo (Ft. Caroline), the one to take the artillery they had captured, and the French women and children, to St. Domingo, and to obtain provisions. The other had to go upon business of his Majesty to other parts.

"'The French captain replied, "that he should grant to all, their lives, and that they should remain with him until they could obtain shipping for France, since they were not at war, and the kings of Spain and of France were brothers and friends." The Adelantado said, "that was true, and Catholics and friends he would favor, believing that he would serve both kings in doing so; but as to themselves, being of the new sect, he held them for enemies, and he would wage war upon them even to blood and to fire; and that he would pursue them with all cruelty wherever he should encounter them, in whatever sea or land where he should be viceroy or captain general for his king; and that he would go and plant the holy faith in this land, that the Indians might be enlightened and be brought to the knowledge of the Holy Catholic Faith of Jesus Christ our Saviour, as taught and announced by the Roman Church. That if they wished to surrender their standards and their arms, and throw themselves upon his mercy, they might do so, for *he would do with them what God should of his grace direct;* or, they could do as they might deem proper; that other treaty or friendship they should not have from him." The French captain replied, that he could not then conclude any other matter with the Adelantado. He went over in the boat, saying, that he went to relate what had passed, and to agree upon what should be done, and within two hours he would return with an answer. The Adelantado said, "They could do as seemed best to them, and he would wait for them." Two hours passed, when the same French captain returned, with those who had accompanied him previously, and said to the General, "that there were many people of family, and nobles among them, and that they would give fifty thousand ducats, of ransom, if he would spare all their lives." He answered, "that although he was a poor soldier, he could not be governed by selfish interests, and if he were to be merciful and lenient, he desired to be so without the suspicion of other motives." The French captain returned to urge the matter. "Do not deceive yourselves," said the Adelantado, "for if Heaven were to join to earth, I would do no otherwise than I have said." The French officer then going towards where his people stood, said, that in accordance with that understanding he would return shortly with an answer; and within half an hour he returned and placed in the boat, the standards, seventy arquebuses, twenty pistols, a quantity of swords and shields, and some helmets and breast-plates; and the captain came to where the General stood, and said that all the French force there submitted themselves to his clemency, and surrendered to him their standards and their arms. The Adelantado then directed twenty soldiers to go in the boat and bring the French, ten by ten. The river was narrow and easy to pass, and he directed Diego Flores de Valdes, Admiral of the Fleet, to receive the standards and the arms, and to go in the boat and see that the soldiers did not maltreat them. The Adelantado then withdrew from the shore, about two bow shots, behind a hillock of sand, within a copse of bushes, where the persons who came in the boat which brought over the French, could not see; and then said to the French captain and the other eight Frenchmen who were there with him, "Gentlemen, I have but few men with me, and they are not very effective, and you are numerous; and, going unrestrained, it would be an easy thing to take satisfaction upon our men for those whom we destroyed when we took the fort; and thus it is necessary that you should march with hands tied behind, a distance of four leagues from here where I have my camp." The French replied "that they would do so;" and they had their hands tied strongly behind their backs with the match ropes of the soldiers; and the ten who came in the boat did not see those who had their hands tied, until they came up to the same place, for it was so arranged, in order that the French who had not passed the river, should not understand what was being done, and might not be offended, and thus were tied two hundred and eight Frenchmen. Of whom the Adelantado asked that if any among them were Catholics, they should declare it. Eight said that they were Catholics, and were separated from the others and placed in a boat, that they might go by the river to St. Augustine; and all the rest replied "that they were of the new religion, and held themselves to be very good Christians; that this was their faith and no other." The Adelantado then gave the order to march with them, having first given them meat and drink, as each ten arrived, before being tied, which was done before the succeeding ten arrived; and he directed one of his captains who marched with the vanguard, that at a certain distance from there he would observe a mark made by a lance, which he carried in his hand, which would be in a sandy place that they would be obliged to pass in going on their way towards the fort of St. Augustine, and that there the prisoners should all be destroyed; and he gave the one in command of the rearguard the same orders; and it was done accordingly; when, leaving there all of the dead, they returned the same night before dawn, to the fort at St. Augustine, although it was already sundown when the men were killed.'"*

Such is the second part of this sad and bloody tragedy; which took place at the Matanzas Inlet, about eighteen miles south of the city of St. Augustine, and at the southerly end of Anastasia Island. The account we have given, it must be borne in mind, is that of De Solis, the brother-in-law and apologist of Menendez; but even under his extenuating hand the conduct of Menendez was that of one deaf to the voice of humanity, and exulting in cold-blooded treachery, dealing in vague generalities intended to deceive, while affording a shallow apology for the actor. A massacre in cold blood of poor shipwrecked, famished men, prisoners yielding themselves to an expected clemency, tied up like sheep, and butchered by poignard blows from behind, shocked alike the moral sense of all to whom the tale came, without regard to faith or flag.

---

* Barcia, p. 87.

CHAPTER VIII.

FATE OF RIBAULT AND HIS FOLLOWERS—BLOODY MASSA-
CRE AT MATANZAS—1565.

The first detachment of the French whom Menendez met and so utterly destroyed, constituted the complement of a single vessel, which had been thrown ashore at a more northerly point than the others. All these vessels were wrecked between Mosquito Inlet and Matanzas.

Of the fate of the main detachment, under Ribault in person, we have the following account, as related by the same apologist, the chaplain De Solis:

"On the next day following the return of the Adelantado at St. Augustine, the same Indians who came before returned, and said that 'a great many more Christians were at the same part of the river as the others had been.' The Adelantado concluded that it must be Jean Ribault, the General of the Lutherans at sea and on land, whom they called the Viceroy of this country for the king of France. He immediately went, with one hundred and fifty men in good order, and reached the place where he had lodged the first time, at about midnight; and at dawn he pushed forward to the river, with his men drawn out, and when it was daylight, he saw, two bow-shots from the other bank of the river, many persons, and a raft made to cross over the people, at the place where the Adelantado stood. But immediately, when the French saw the Adelantado and his people, they took arms, and displayed a royal standard and two standards of companies, sounding fifes and drums, in very good order, and showing a front of battle to the Adelantado; who, having ordered his men to sit down and take their breakfast, so that they made no demonstration of any change, he himself walked up and down the shore, with his admiral and two other captains, paying no attention to the movement and demonstration of battle of the French; so that they observing this, halted and the fifes and the drums ceased, while with a bugle note they unfurled the white flag of peace, which was returned by the Adelantado. A Frenchman placed himself upon the raft, and cried with a loud voice that he wished to cross over, but that owing to the force of the current he could not bring the raft over, and desired an Indian canoe which was there to be sent over. The Adelantado said he could swim over for it, under pledge of his word. A French sailor immediately came over, but the General would not permit him to speak with him, but directed him to take the canoe, and go and tell his captain, that inasmuch as he called for a conference, if he desired anything he should send over some one to communicate with him. The same sailor immediately came with a gentleman, who said he was the sergeant major of Jean Ribault, Viceroy and Captain General of this land for the king of France, and that he had sent him to say, that they had been wrecked with their fleet in a great storm, and that he had with him three hundred and fifty French; that they wished to go to a fort which they held, twenty leagues from there; that they wished the favor of boats, to pass this river, and the other, four leagues further on, and that he desired to know if they were Spaniards, and under what leader they served.

"The Adelantado answered him, that they were Spaniards, and that the captain under whom they served was the person now addressing him, and was called Pedro Menendez. That he should tell his General that the fort which he held twenty leagues from there had been taken by him, and he had destroyed all the French, and the rest who had come with the fleet, because they were badly governed; and then, passing thence to where the dead bodies of the Frenchmen whom he had killed still lay unburied, pointed them out to him and said, therefore he could not permit them to pass the river to their fort.

"The sergeant, with an unmoved countenance, and without any appearance of uneasiness on account of what the Adelantado had said, replied, that if he would have the goodness to send a gentleman of his party, to say to the French general, that they might negotiate with safety, the people were much exhausted, and the general would come over in a boat which was there. The Adelantado replied, 'Farewell, comrade, and bear the answer which they shall give you; and if your general desires to come and treat with me, I give my word that he shall come and return securely, with four or six of his people whom he may select for his advisors, that he may do whatever he may conclude to be best.'

"The French gentleman then departed with this message. Within half an hour he returned to accept the assurance the

Adelantado had given, and to obtain the boat; which the Adelantado was unwilling to let him have, but said he could use the canoe, which was safe, and the strait was narrow: and he again went back with this message.

"Immediately Jean Ribault came over, whom the Adelantado received very well, with other eight gentleman, who had come with him. They were all gentlemen of rank and position. He gave them a collation, and would have given them food if they had desired. Jean Ribault with much humility, thanked him for his kind reception, and said that to raise their spirits, much depressed by the sad news of the death of their comrades, they would partake only of the wine and condiments, and did not wish anything else to eat. Then after eating, Jean Ribault said, 'that he saw that those his companions were dead, and that he could not be mistaken if he desired to be.' Then the Adelantado directed the soldiers to bring each one whatever he had taken from the fort; and he saw so many things that he knew for certain that it was taken: although he knew this before, yet he could not wholly believe it, because among his men there was a Frenchman by name of Barbero, of those whom the Adelantado had ordered to be destroyed with the rest, and was left for dead with the others, having with the first thrust he received fallen down and made as though he were dead, and when they left there he had passed over by swimming, to Ribault; and this Barbero held it for certain that the Adelantado had deceived them in saying that the fort was taken, it not being so; and thus until now he had supposed. The Adelantado said that in order with more certainty to believe this and satisfy himself, he might converse apart with the two Frenchmen who were present, to satisfy him better: which he did.

"Immediately Jean Ribault came towards the Adelantado and said, 'it was certain that all which he had told him was true; but that what had happened to him, might have happened to the Adelantado: and since their kings were brothers, and such great friends, the Adelantado should act towards him as a friend, and give him ships and provisions, that he might return to France.'

"The Adelantado replied in the same manner that he had done to the other Frenchmen, as to what he would do; and that taking it or leaving it, Jean Ribault could obtain nothing further from the Adelantado. Jean Ribault then said that he would go and give an account of matters to his people, for he had among them many of noble blood; and would return or send an answer as to what he would do.

"Three hours afterwards, Jean Ribault returned in the canoe, and said, 'that there were different opinions among his people; that while some were willing to yield themselves to his clemency, others were not.' The Adelantado replied 'that it mattered but little to him whether they all came, or a part, or none at all; that they should do as it pleased them, and he would act with the same liberty.' Jean Ribault said to him, 'that the half of the people who were willing to yield themselves to his clemency, would pay him a ransom of more than 100,000 ducats; and the other half were able to pay more, for there were among them persons of wealth and large incomes, who had desired to establish estates in this country.' The Adelantado answered him, 'It would grieve me much to lose so great and rich a ransom, under the necessity I am under for such aid, to carry forward the conquest and settlement of this land, in the name of my king, as is my duty, and to plant here the Holy Evangel.' Jean Ribault considered from this, that with the amount they could all give, he might be induced to spare his own life and that of all the others who were with him, and that they might be able to pay more than 200,000 ducats; and he said to the Adelantado, 'that he would return with his answer to his people; that as it was late, he would take it as a favor if he would be willing to wait until the following day, when he would bring their reply as to what they would conclude to do.' The Adelantado said, 'Yes, that he would wait.' Jean Ribault then went back to his people, it being already sunset. In the morning, he returned with the canoe, and surrendered to the Adelantado two royal standards—the one that of the king of France, the other that of the Admiral (Coligny),—and the standards of the company, and a sword, dagger, and helmet, gilded very beautifully; and also a shield, a pistol, and a commission given him under the high admiral of France, to assure to him his title and possessions.

"He then said to him, 'that but one hundred and fifty of the three hundred and fifty whom he had with him were willing to yield to his clemency, and that the others had withdrawn during the night; and that they might take the boat and bring those who were willing to come over, and their arms.' The Adelantado immediately directed the captain, Diego Flores Valdes, Admiral of the fleet, that he should bring them over as he had done the others, ten by
4

ten; and the Adelantado, taking Jean Ribault behind the sand hills, among the bushes where the others had their hands tied behind them, he said to these and all the others as he had done before, that they had four leagues to go after night, and that he could not permit them to go unbound; and after they were all tied, he asked if they were Catholics or Lutherans, or if any of them desired to make confession.

"Jean Ribault replied, 'that all who were there were of the new religion,' and he then began to repeat the psalm, 'Domine! Memento! Mei;' and having finished, he said, 'that from dust they came and to dust they must return, and that in twenty years, more or less, he must render his final account; that the Adelantado might do with them as he chose.' The Adelantado then ordered all to be killed, in the same order and at the same mark, as had been done to the others. He spared only the fifers, drummers, and trumpeters, and four others who said that they were Catholics, in all, sixteen persons." "*Todos los demas fueron degollados*,"—"all the rest were slaughtered," is the sententious summary by which Padre de Solis announced the close of the sad career of the gray-haired veteran, the brave soldier, the Admiral Jean Ribault, and his companions.*

At some point on the thickly-wooded shores of the Island of Anastasio, or beneath the shifting mounds of sand which mark its shores, may still lie the bones of some of the three hundred and fifty who, spared from destruction by the tempest, and escaping the perils of the sea and of the savage, fell victims to the vindictive rancor and blind rage of one than whom history recalls none more cruel, or less humane. But while their bones, scattered on earth and sea, unhonored and unburied, were lost to human sight, the tale of their destruction and sad fate, scattered in like manner over the whole world, has raised to their memory through sympathy with their fate, a memorial which will endure as long as the pages of history.

The Adelantado returned that night to St. Augustine, where, says his apologist, some persons censured him for his cruelty. Others commended what he had done, as the act of a good general, and said that even if they had been Catholics, he could not have done more justly than he had done for them; for with the few provisions that the Adelantado had, either the one or the other people would have had to perish with hunger, and the French would have destroyed our people: they were the most numerous.†

---

* Barcia, p. 89.   † Barcia, p. 89.

OF ST. AUGUSTINE, FLORIDA.   51

We have still to trace the fate of the body of two hundred, who retired from Ribault after his final determination to surrender to the tender mercies of Menendez. As we are already aware, it comprised the elite of his force, men of standing and rank, and whose spirits had retained energy to combat against the natural discouragements of their position; and they adopted the nobler resolve of selling their lives, at least with their swords in their hands.

De Solis proceeds to give the following further account of them:—

"Twenty days subsequently to the destruction of these, some Indians came to the Adelantado, and informed him by signs, that eight days' journey from here to the southward, near the Bahama Channel, at Canaveral, a large number of people, brethren of those whom the General had caused to be killed, were building a fort and a vessel. The Adelantado at once came to the conclusion, that the French had retired to the place where their vessels were wrecked, and where their artillery and munitions, and provisions were, in order to build a vessel and return to France to procure succor. The General thereupon dispatched from St. Augustine to St. Matteo, ten of his soldiers, conveying intelligence of what had taken place, and directing that they should send to him one hundred and fifty of the soldiers there, with the thirty-five others who remained when he returned to St. Augustine, after taking the fort. The master of the camp immediately dispatched them, under command of Captains Juan Velez de Medrano and Andrez Lopez Patrio; and they arrived at St. Augustine on October 23d. On the 25th, after having heard mass, the Adelantado departed for the coast, with three hundred men, and three small vessels to go by sea with the arms and provisions; and the vessels were to go along and progress equally with the troops; and each night when the troops halted, the vessels also anchored by them, for it was a clear and sandy coast.

"The Adelantado carried in the three vessels provisions for forty days for three hundred men, and one day's ration was to last for two days; and he promised to do everything for the general good of all, although they might have to undergo many dangers and privations; that he had great hope that he would have the goodness and mercy of God to aid him in carrying through safely this so holy and pious an undertaking. He then took leave of them, leaving most of them in tears, for he was much loved, feared, and respected by all.*

---

* Barcia, p. 89.

"The Adelantado, after a wearisome journey, marching on foot himself the whole distance, arrived in the neighborhood of the French camp on All Saints Day, at daylight, guided by the Indians by land, and the three vessels under the command of Captain Diego de Maya. As soon as the French descried the Spaniards, they fled to their fort, without any remaining. The Adelantado sent them a trumpeter, offering them their lives, that they should return and should receive the same treatment as the Spaniards. One hundred and fifty came to the Adelantado; and their leader, with twenty others, sent to say that they would sooner be devoured by the Indians, than surrender themselves to the Spaniards. The Adelantado received those who surrendered, very well, and having set fire to the fort, which was of wood, burned the vessel which they were building, and buried the artillery, for the vessels could not carry them."

De Solis here closes his account of the matter; but from other accounts we learn that the Adelantado kept his faith on this occasion with them, and that some entered his service, some were converted to his faith, and others returned to France; and thus ended the Huguenot attempt to colonize the shores of Florida.

There are several other accounts of the fate of Ribault and his followers, drawn from the narratives of survivors of the expedition, which, without varying the general order of events, fill in sundry details of the massacres. The main point of difference is, as to the pledges or assurances given by Menendez. The French accounts say that he pledged his faith to them that their lives should be spared.* It will be seen that the Spanish account denies that he did so, but makes him use language subject to misconstruction, and calculated to deceive them into the hope and expectation of safety. I do not see that in a Christian or even moral view there is much difference between an open breach of faith and the breach of an implied faith, particularly when it was only by this deception that the surrender could have been accomplished. Nor could Menendez have had a very delicate sense of the value of the word of a soldier, a Christian, and a gentleman, when, as his apologist admits, he did directly use the language of falsehood, to induce them to submit to the degradation of having their hands tied.

Nor, considered in its broader aspects, is it a matter of any

---

* Such was the understanding of those who then wrote in reference to the transaction, as Barcia admits.

consequence whether he gave his word or no; nor does it lessen the enormity of his conduct, had they submitted themselves in the most unreserved manner to his discretion. France and Spain were at peace; no act of hostility had been committed by the French toward the Spaniards; and Ribault asked only to be allowed to pass on. In violation alike of the laws of war and the law of humanity, he first induced them to surrender, to abide what God, whose holy name he invoked, should put into his heart to do, and then cajoling them into allowing their hands to be tied, he ordered them to be killed, in their bonds as they stood, defenseless, helpless, wrecked, and famished men. It would have been a base blot upon human nature, had he thus served the most savage tribe of nations, standing on that far shore, brought into the common sympathy of want and suffering. The act seems one of monstrous atrocity, when committed against the people of a sister nation.

CHAPTER IX.

FORTIFYING OF ST. AUGUSTINE—DISAFFCTIONS AND MUTINIES—APPROVAL OF MENENDEZ' ACTS BY THE KING OF SPAIN. 1565-1568.

During the time of the several expeditions of the Adelantado against the French Huguenots, the fortification and strengthening of the defenses of the settlement at St. Augustine had not been neglected. The fort, or Indian council-house, which had been first fortified, seems to have been consumed in the conflagration spoken of; and thereupon a plan of a regular fortification or fort was marked out by Menendez; and, as there existed some danger of the return of the French, the Spaniards labored unceasingly with their whole force, to put it in a respectable state of defense. From an engraving contained in De Bry, illustrating the attack of Sir Francis Drake, twenty years afterwards, this fort appears to have been an octagonal structure of logs, and located near the site of the present fort, while the settlement itself was probably made in the first instance, at the lower end of the peninsula, near the building now called "the powder-house."

He also established a government for the place, with civil and military officials, a hall of justice, etc.

All of these matters were arranged by Menendez before his expedition against the French at Canaveral, of whom one hundred and fifty returned with him, and were received upon an equal footing with his own men, the more distinguished being received at his own table upon the most friendly terms; a clemency which, with a knowledge of his character, can only be ascribed to motives of policy. The position of the French at Canaveral was probably inaccessible, as they had their arms, besides artillery brought from the vessels; and the duplicity which had characterized his success with their comrades, was out of the question here; the French could therefore exact their own terms, and unshackled could forcibly resist any attempt at treachery.

The addition of this number to his force lessened the already diminished supply of provisions which Menendez had brought with him; and want soon began to threaten his camp. He sent as many of his soldiers as he could into camp at San Matteo, and endeavored to draw supplies from the Indians; but unfortunately for him, the country between the St. Johns and St. Augustine was under the rule of the Indian Chief, Satouriara, the friend (and ally of the French), whose hostility the Spaniards were never able to overcome. Satouriara and his followers withdrew from all peaceable intercourse with the Spaniards, and hung about their path to destroy, harrass, and cut them off upon every possible occasion.

The winter succeeding the settlement of the Spaniards at St. Augustine, was most distressing and discouraging to them. The lack of provisions in their camp drove them to seek, in the surrounding country, subsistence from the roots and esculent plants it might afford, or to obtain in the neighboring creeks, fish and oysters; but no sooner did a Spaniard venture out alone beyond the gates of the fort, than he was grasped, by some unseen foe, from the low underbrush and put to death, or a shower of arrows from some tree-top was his first intimation of danger; if he discharged his arquebuse towards his invisible assailants, others would spring upon him before he could reload his piece; or, if he attempted to find fish and oysters in some quiet creek, the noiseless canoe of an Indian would dart in upon him, and the heavy war-club of the savage descending upon his unprotected head, end his existence. Against such a foe, no defense could avail; and it is related that more than one hundred and twenty of the Spaniards were thus killed, including Captain Martin de Ochoa, Captain Diego de Hevia, Fernando de Gamboa, and Juan Menendez, a nephew of the Adelantado, and many others of the bravest and most distinguished of the garrison.

In this crisis of affairs, the Governor concluded to go to Cuba himself, to obtain relief for his colony. He in the meantime established a fort at St. Lucia, near Canaveral. A considerable jealousy seems to have existed on the part of the governor of Cuba; and he received Menendez with great coolness, and in reply to his appeals for aid, only offered an empty vessel. In this emergency, Menendez contemplated, as his only means of obtaining what he wished, to go upon a filibustering expedition against some Portuguese and English vessels which were in those waters. While making preparations to do this, four vessels of the fleet with which he had left Spain, and which had been supposed lost, arrived; and after dispatching a vessel to Campeachy for provisions, he commenced his return voyage to his colony, delaying however for a time in South Florida, to seek intelligence among the Indians of his lost son.

In the meantime his garrisons at St. Augustine and San Matteo had mutinied, and were in open revolt; provisions had become so scarce that twenty-five reals had been given for a pound of biscuit, and but for the fish they would have starved. They plundered the public stores, imprisoned their officers, and seized upon a vessel laden with provisions which had been sent to the garrison. The Master of the Camp succeeded in escaping from confinement and releasing his fellow prisoners, by a bold movement cut off the intercourse between the mutineers on board the vessel and those on shore, and hung the Sergeant Major, who was at the head of the movement. The Commandant then attempted to attack those in the vessel, and was nearly lost with his companions, by being wrecked on the bar. The vessel made sail to the West India Islands. The garrison at San Matteo took a vessel there and come around to St. Augustine, but arrived after their accomplices had left.

Disease had already begun to make its ravages, and added to the general wish to leave the country; which all would then have done had they had the vessels in which to embark. They used for their recovery from sickness, the roots of a native shrub, which produced marvelous cures.

At this period Menendez returned to the famished garrison, but was forced to permit Juan Vicente, with one hundred of the disaffected, to go to St. Domingo by a vessel which he dispatched there for supplies; and it is said that the governors of the islands where they went, harbored them, and that of some five hundred who on different occasions deserted from the Adelantado, and all of whom had been brought out at his cost, but two or three were ever returned to him; while the deserters putting their own construction upon their acts, sent home to the king of Spain criminations of the Adelantado, and represented the conquest of Florida as a hopeless and worthless acquisition; that it was barren and swampy, and produced nothing.

After this defection, Menendez proceeded along the coast to San Matteo, and thence to Guale, Amelia, and adjoining islands. Orista and St. Helena; made peaceful proposals to the Indian tribes, lectured them upon theology, and planted a cross at their council-houses. The cacique of Guale asked Menendez how it was "that he had waged war upon the other white men, who had come from the same country as himself?" He replied, "that the other white people were bad Christians, and believers in lies; and that those whom he had killed, deserved the most cruel death, because they had fled their own country, and came to mislead and deceive the caciques and other Indians, as they had already before misled and deceived many other good Christians, in order that the devil may take possession of them." While at St. Helena he succeeded in obtaining permission of the Indians to erect a fort there, and he left a detachment. On his return he also erected fort San Felipe, at Orista; and after setting up a cross at Guale, the cacique demanded of him, that as now they had become good Christians, he should cause rain to come upon their fields; for a drought had continued eight months. The same night a severe rain-storm happened, which confirmed the faith of the Indians, and gained the Adelantado great credit with them. While here, he learned that there was a fugitive Lutheran among the Indians, and he took some pains to cause to be given to the fugitive hopes of good treatment if he would come into the Spanish post at St. Helena, while he gave private directions that he should be killed, directing his lieutenant to make very strange of his disappearance; an incident very illustrative of the vindictiveness and duplicity of Menendez.*

He returned to St. Augustine, and was received with great joy, and devoted himself to the completion of the fort, which was to frighten the savages, and enforce respect from strangers. It was built, it is said, where it now stands, *donde este ahora*, (1722.)

The colony left at St. Helena mutinied almost immediately, and seizing a vessel sent with supplies, sailed for Cuba, and were wrecked on the Florida Keys, where they met at an Indian town the mutineers who had deserted from the fort at St. Matteo: these had been also wrecked there.

The garrison again becoming much straitened for provisions, the Adelantado, in June, was obliged to go to Cuba for succor. He was received with indifference, and his wishes unheeded. He applied to the governor of Mexico, and others who happened to be there, and who had the power of assisting him; from all he received no encouragement, but the advice to abandon his enterprise. He at last pawned his jewels, the badge of his order, and his valuables, thus obtaining five hundred ducats; with which he purchased provisions, and set sail on his return, with only sixty-five men.

But just at this period succor came to the famished

---

* Ensay. Cron. 110.

troops: a fleet of seventeen vessels arrived with fifteen hundred men from Spain, under Juan de Avila, as admiral. By this means all the posts were succored and reinforced, and the enterprise saved from destruction; for the small supplies brought by Menendez would have been soon exhausted, and further efforts being out of his power, they would have been forced to withdraw from the country.

The admiral of the fleet also had entrusted to him for the Adelantado a letter from the king, written on the 12th of May, 1566, which, among other matters, contained the following royal commendation of the acts of Menendez. "Of the great success which has attended your enterprise, we have the most entire satisfaction, and we bear in memory the loyalty, the love, and the diligence, with which you have borne us service, as well as the dangers and perils in which you have been placed; and as to the *retribution* you have visited upon the Lutheran pirates who sought to occupy that country, and to fortify themselves there, in order to disseminate in it their wicked creed, and to prosecute there their wrongs and robberies, which they have done and were doing against God's service and my own, we believe that you did it with every justification and propriety, and we consider ourself to have been well served in so doing."*

To this commendation of Philip II., it is unnecessary to add any comment, save that no other action could have been expected of him. And of Charles the Ninth, of France, the Spanish historian says that he treated the memorial of the widows and orphans of the slain with contempt, "considering their punishment to have been just, in that they were equally enemies of Spain, of France, of the Church, and of the peace of the world."

During the absence of Menendez to inspect his posts, disaffection again broke out; and finding his force too numerous, he with sixteen vessels went upon a freebooting expedition to attack pirates. He failed to meet with any; but having learned that a large French fleet was on its way, he visited and fortified the forts on the islands of Cuba, Hispaniola, and Puerto Rico, and again returned to Florida; the expected French fleet never having arrived. About this time, a small vessel brought from Spain three learned and exemplary priests; one of whom, Padre Martinez, landed upon the coast with some of the crew, and being unable to regain the vessel, coasted along to St. George

---

* Ensayo: Cron. 115.

Island, where he was attacked and murdered by the Indians, with a number of his companions.

The following year was principally occupied by Menendez, n strengthening his fortifications at his three forts, in visiting the Indian chiefs at their towns, and exploring the country. One of his expeditions went as far north as the thirty-seventh degree of latitude by sea, and another went to the foot of the Apalachian Mountains, about one hundred and fifty leagues, and established a fort. The former was about the mouth of the Chesapeake, called the Santa Maria,* and the land expedition, probably to the up-country of Georgia, in the neighborhood of Rome.

All attempts at pacifying their warlike neighbor were as fruitless as their attempts to subjugate him; whether in artifice and duplicity, in open warfare, or secret ambush, he was more than equal to the Adelantado, and was a worthy ancestor of the modern Seminole,—never present when looked for, and never absent when an opportunity of striking a blow occurred.

The Adelantado having had built an extremely slight vessel of less than twenty tons, called a frigate, concluded to visit Spain, and ran in seventeen days to the Azores, sailing seventy leagues per day, an exploit not often equaled in modern times. He was received with great joy in Spain, and the king treated him with much consideration. The Adelantado felt great anxiety to return to his colony, and deprecated the delays of the court, fearing the result of the indignation at his cruelty to the Huguenots, which, says his chronicler, increased day by day.†

---

* Pensacola Bay was also so called.

† Ensayo: Cron. 133.

CHAPTER X.

THE NOTABLE REVENGE OF DOMINIC DE GOURGUES—RETURN OF MENENDEZ—INDIAN MISSION—1568.

While Menendez thus remained at the Spanish court urging the completion of his business, seeking compensation for the great expenditures which he had made in the king's service, and vindicating himself from the accusations which had been preferred against him,—the revenge, the distant murmurs of which had already reached his ears, fell upon the Spaniards on the St. Johns.

Dominic de Gourgues, one of those soldiers of fortune who then abounded throughout Europe, took upon himself the expression of the indignation with which the French nation viewed the slaughter of their countrymen. From motives of policy, or from feelings still less creditable, the French court ignored the event; but it rankled nevertheless in the national heart, and many a secret vow of revenge was breathed, the low whispers of which reached even the confines of the Spanish court. Conscience, and the knowledge that the sentiment of the age was against him, made Menendez from the moment of his success exceedingly anxious lest well-merited retribution should fall upon his own colony. He guarded against it in every way in his power; he strengthened all his posts; he erected for the protection of San Matteo, formerly Fort Caroline, two small forts on either side of the entrance of the river, at the points now known as Batten Island and Mayport Mills. He placed large garrisons at each post, and had made such arrangements against surprise or open attack upon his forts, that Father Mendoza boasted that "half of all France could not take them."

De Gourgues, with three vessels and about two hundred and fifty chosen men, animated with like feelings with himself, appeared in April, 1568, off the mouth of the St. Johns. The Spanish fort received his vessels with a salute, supposing them to be under the flag of Spain. De Gourgues returned the salute, thus confirming their error. He then entered the St. Marys, called the Somme, and was met by a large concourse of Indians, friendly to the French and bitterly hostile to the Spaniards, at the head of whom was the stern and uncompromising Saturioura. Their plans were quickly formed, and immediately carried into execution. Their place of rendezvous was the Fort George Inlet, called by them the Sarabay; and they traversed that island at low tide, fell suddenly upon the fort at Batten Island on the north side of the river, completely surprising it. The force occupying the Spanish forts amounted to four hundred men, one hundred and twenty of whom occupied the two forts at the mouth of the river, and the remainder Fort Caroline. The French with their Indian allies approached the fort on the north side of the river at day-break. Having waded the intervening marsh and creek, to the great damage of their feet and legs by reason of the oyster banks, they arrived within two hundred yards of the post, when they were discovered by the sentinel upon the platform of the fort; who immediately cried, "to arms," and discharged twice at the French a culverin which had been taken at Fort Caroline. Before he could load it a third time the brave Olatocara leaped upon him, and killed him with a pike. Gourgues then charging in, the garrison, by this time alarmed, rushed out, armed hastily and seeking escape; another part of Gourgues' force coming up, inclosed the Spaniards between them, and all but fifteen of the garrison perished on the spot; the others were taken prisoners, only to be reserved for the summary vengeance which the French leader meditated.

The Spanish garrison in the other fort kept up in the mean time a brisk cannonade, which incommoded the assailants, who however soon managed to point the pieces of the fort they had taken; and under the cover of this fire the French crossed to the other fort, their Indian allies in great numbers swimming with them. The garrison of sixty men, panic-struck, made no attempt at resistance, but fled, endeavoring to reach the main fort; being intercepted by the Indians in one direction, and by the French in another, but few made good their escape. These, arriving at Fort Caroline, carried an exaggerated account of the number of their assailants.

De Gourgues at once pushed forward to attack Fort Caroline, while its defenders were terrified at the suddenness of his attack, and the supposed strength of his force. Upon his arrival near the fort, the Spanish commander sent out a detachment of sixty men, to make a reconnoisance. De Gourgues skilfully interposed a body of his own men with a large number of the Indians between the reconnoitering party and the fort, and then with his main force charged upon them in front; when the Spaniards, turning to seek the shelter of the fort, were met by the force in their rear, and were all either killed or taken prisoners. Seeing this misfortune, the Spanish commander despaired of being able to hold the fortress, and determined to make a timely retreat to St. Augustine. In attempting this, most of his followers fell into the hands of the Indians, and were slain upon the spot; the commandant with a few others alone escaped.

De Gourgues, now completely successful in making retaliation for the fate of his countrymen on the same spot where they suffered, on the same tree which had borne the bodies of the Huguenots caused his prisoners to be suspended; and as Menedez had on the former occasion erected a tablet that they had been punished "not as Frenchmen but as Lutherans," so De Gourgues in like manner erected an inscription that he had done this to them "*not as to Spaniards, nor as to outcasts, but as to traitors, thieves and murderers.*"*

After inducing the Indians to destroy the forts, and to raze them to the ground, he set sail for France, arriving safely without further adventure.

His conduct was at the time disavowed and censured by the French court; and the Spanish ambassador had the assurance, in the name of that master who had publicly declared his approval of the conduct of Menendez, to demand the surrender of De Gourgues to his vengence. The brave captain, however the crown might seem to disapprove, was secretly sustained and protected by many distinguished persons official and private, and by the mass of the people; to whom his boldness, spirit, and signal success were grateful. Some years afterwards he was restored to the favor of his sovereign, and appointed admiral of the fleet.

That De Gourgues deserves censure, cannot be denied; but there will always exist an admiration for his courage and intrepid valor, with a sympathy for the bitter provocations under which he acted, both personal and national; a sympathy not shared with Menendez, who visited his wrath upon the religious opinions of men, while De Gourgues was the unauthorized avenger of undoubted crime and inhumanity. Both acted in violation of the pure spirit of that

---

* Ternaux Compans, p. 357.

Christianity which they alike professed to revere, under the same form.

While these scenes were enacting on the St. Johns, Menendez was on his way to his colonies, where he first heard of the descent of De Gourgues, then on his way back to France. The Adelantado upon his arrival found his troops hungry and naked, and their relations with the Indians worse than ever. Having made such arrangements as were in his power, he returned to Havana, to further his plans for introducing Christianity among the Indians; to which, to his credit be it said, he devoted the greater share of his time and attention. Father Rogel applied himself to learning their language, with great success; and an institution was established in Havana especially for their instruction. In the Ensayo Cronologica, there is set forth in full, a rescript addressed by Pope Pius V., to Menendez, conveying to him the acknowledgements of his Holiness for the zeal and loyalty he had exhibited, and his labors in carrying the faith to the Indians, and urging him strongly to see to it that his Indian converts should not be scandalized by the vicious lives of their white brethren who claimed to be Christians.

A small party of Spaniards, as has already been mentioned, accompanied by a priest, De Quiros, had been left upon the Chesapeake, and under the auspices of a young converted chief, who had been some time with the Spaniards in Havana and Florida, anticipated a more easy access to the Indian tribes in that region. Another priest, with ten associates, went the following year; when, after they had sent away their vessel, they discovered that their predecessor had been murdered, through the treachery of the renegade apostate; and they themselves shortly fell victims to his perfidy. Menendez dispatched a third vessel there; when the fate of the two former parties was ascertained, and he went in person to chastise the murderers; he succeeded in capturing six or seven, who, it is said, (rather improbably I think), confessed themselves to have been implicated in the massacre. Menendez, in his summary and sailor-like way, ordered their execution at the yard-arm of his vessel. The Cronicle says that they were first converted and baptized, by the zeal of Farther Rogel, before the sentence was carried into execution. A long period elapsed before any further efforts were made in this quarter to establish a colony; and it was then accomplished by the English. In consequence of these temporary establishments, however, the

Spanish crown, for a long period, claimed the whole of the intervening country, as lying within its Province of Florida.

The annals of the city during the remainder of the life of Menendez, present only the usual vicissitudes of new settlements,—the alternations of supply and want, occasional disaffections, and petty annoyances.

Menendez was the recipient from his court of new honors from time to time, and had been appointed the grand admiral of the Spanish Armada; when, in September, 1574, he was suddenly carried off by a fever, at the age of fifty-five. It is a singular coincidence that De Gourgues, five years afterwards, was carried off in a similar manner, just after his appointment as admiral of the French fleet. A splendid monument in the church of San Nicolas, at Aviles, was erected to the memory of Menendez, with the following inscription:

"HERE LIES BURIED THE ILLUSTRIOUS CAVALIER, PEDRO MENENDEZ DE AVILES, A NATIVE OF THIS CITY, ADELANTADO OF THE PROVINCES OF FLORIDA, KNIGHT COMMANDER OF SANTA CRUZ OF THE ORDER OF SANTIAGO, AND CAPTAIN GENERAL OF THE OCEANIC SEAS AND OF THE ARMADA WHICH HIS ROYAL HIGHNESS COLLECTED AT SANTANDER IN THE YEAR 1574, WHERE HE DIED ON THE 17TH OF SEPTEMBER OF THAT YEAR, IN THE 55TH YEAR OF HIS AGE."

CHAPTER XI.

SIR FRANCIS DRAKE'S ATTACK UPON ST. AUGUSTINE—
ESTABLISHMENT OF MISSIONS—MASSACRE OF MISSION-
ARIES AT ST. AUGUSTINE—1586-1638.

Nine years had elapsed from the death of Menendez, and the colony at St. Augustine had slowly progressed into the settlement of a small town; but the eclat and importance which the presence of Menendez had given it, were much lessened; when, in 1586, Sir Francis Drake, with a fleet returning from South America, discovered the Spanish look-out upon Anastasia Island, and sent boats ashore to ascertain something in reference to it. Marching up the shore, they discovered across the bay, a fort, and further up a town built of wood.

Proceeding towards the fort, which bore the name of San Juan de Pinas, some guns were fired upon them from it, and they retired towards their vessel; the same evening a fifer made his appearance, and informed them that he was a Frenchman, detained a prisoner there, and that the Spaniards had abandoned their fort; and he offered to conduct them over. Upon this information they crossed the river and found the fort abandoned as they had been informed, and took possession of it without opposition. It was built entirely of wood, and only surrounded by a wall or pale formed of the bodies or trunks of large trees, set upright in the earth; for, says the narrative, it was not at that time inclosed by a ditch, as it had been but lately begun by the Spaniards. The platforms were made of the bodies of large pine trees (of which there are plenty here), laid horizontally across each other, with earth rammed in to fill up the vacancies. Fourteen brass cannon were found in the fort, and there was left behind the treasure chest, containing £2,000 sterling, designed for the payment of the garrison, which consisted of one hundred and fifty men. Whether the massive, iron-bound mahogany chest,* still preserved in the old fort is the same which fell into the

---

* This old chest, which remained in one of the western vaults of the fort, up to the late war, was broken up for relics, and is no longer there.

hands of Drake, is a question for antiquaries to decide; its ancient appearance might well justify the supposition.

On the following day, Drake's forces marched towards the town, but owing, it is said, to heavy rains, were obliged to return and go in the boats. On their approach, the Spaniards fled into the country. It is said, in Barcia, that a Spaniard concealed in the bushes, fired at the sergeant major and wounded him, and then ran up and dispatched him, and that in revenge for this act, Drake burnt their buildings and destroyed their gardens. The garrison and inhabitants retired to fort San Matteo, on the St. Johns river. Barcia says that the population of the place was then increasing considerably, and that it possessed a hall of justice, parochial church, and other buildings, together with gardens in the rear of the town.

An engraved plan or view of Drake's descent upon St. Augustine, published after his return to England, represents an octagonal fort between two streams; at the distance of half a mile another stream; beyond that the town, with a look-out and two religious houses, one of which is a church, and the other probably the house of the Franciscans, who had shortly before established a house of their order there. The town contains three squares lengthwise, and four in width, with gardens on the west side.

Some doubt has been thrown on the actual site of the first settlement, by this account; but I think it probably stood considerably to the south of the present public square, between the barracks and the powder-house. Perhaps the Maria Sanchez creek may have then communicated with the bay near its present head, in wet weather and at high tides isolating the fort from the town. The present north ditch may have been the bed of a tide creek, and thus would correspond to the appearance presented by the sketch. It is well known that the north end of the city was built at a much later period than the southern, and that the now vacant space below the barracks, was once occupied with buildings. Buildings and fields are shown upon Anastasia Island, opposite the town. The relative position of the town with reference to the entrance of the harbor is correctly shown on the plan; and there seems no sufficient ground to doubt the identity of the present town with the ancient locality.

The garrison and country were then under the command of Don Pedro Menendez, a nephew of the Adelantado, who, after the English squadron sailed, having received assistance from Havana, began, it is said, to rebuild the city, and made great efforts to increase its population, and to induce the Indians to settle in its neighborhood.

In 1592, twelve Franciscan missionaries arrived at St. Augustine, with their Superior, Fray Joan de Silva, and placed themselves under the charge of Father Francis Manou, Warden of the convent of St. Helena. One of them, a Mexican, Farther Francis Panja, drew up in the language of the Yemasees his "Abridgment of Christian Doctrine," said to be the first work compiled in any of our Indian languages.

The Franciscan Father Corpa established a Mission house for the Indians at Talomato, in the northwest portion of the city of St. Augustine, where there was than an Indian village. Father Blas de Rodriguez, also called Montes, had an Indian Church at a village of the Indians, called Tapoqui, situated on the creek called Cano de la Leche, north of the fort; and the church bearing the name of "Our Lady of the Milk" was situated on the elevated ground a quarter of a mile north of the fort, near the creek. A stone church existed at this locality as late as 1795, and the crucifix belonging to it is preserved in the Roman Catholic Church at St. Augustine.

These missions proceeded with considerable apparent success, large numbers of the Indians being received and instructed both at this and other missions.

Among the converts at the mission of Talomato, was the son of the cacique of the province of Guale, a proud and high-spirited young leader, who by no means submitted to the requirements of his spiritual fathers, but indulged in excesses which scandalized his profession. Father Corpa, after trying private remonstrances and warnings in vain, thought it necessary to administer to him a public rebuke. This aroused the pride of the young chief, and he suddenly left the mission, determined upon revenge. He gathered from the interior a band of warriors, whom he inspired with his own hatred against the missionaries. Returning to Talomato with his followers under the cover of night, he crept up to the mission house, burst open the chapel doors, and slew the devoted Father Corpa while at prayer; then severed his head from his body, set it upon a pikestaff, and threw his body out into the forest where it could never afterwards be found. The scene of this tragedy was in the neighborhood of the present Roman Catholic cemetery of St. Augustine.

As soon as this occurence became known in the Indian

village, all was excitement; some of the most devoted bewailing the death of their spiritual father, while others dreaded the consequences of so rash an act, and shrunk with terror from the vengeance of the Spaniards, which they foresaw would soon follow. The young chief of Guale gathered them around him, and in earnest tones addressed them. "Yes," said he, "the friar is dead. It would not have been done, if he would have allowed us to live as we did before we became Christians. We desire to return to our ancient customs; and we must provide for our defense against the punishment which will be hurled upon us by the Governor of Florida, which, if it be allowed to reach us, will be as rigorous for this single friar, as if we had killed them all.— For the same power which we possess to destroy this one priest, we have to destroy them all."

His followers approved of what had been done, and said there was no doubt but what the same vengeance would fall upon them for the death of the one, as for all.

He then resumed. "Since we shall receive equal punishment for the death of this one, as though we had killed them all, let us regain the liberty of which these friars have robbed us, with their promises of good things which we have not yet seen, but which they seek to keep us in hope of, while they accumulate upon us who are called Christians, injuries and disgusts, making us quit our wives, restricting us to one only, and prohibiting us from changing her.— They prevent us from having our balls, banquets, feasts, celebrations, games and contests, so that being deprived of them, we lose our ancient valor and skill which we inherited from our ancestors. Although they oppress us with labor, refusing to grant even the respite of a few days, and although we are disposed to do all they require from us, they are not satisfied; but for everything they reprimand us, injuriously treat us, oppress us, lecture us, call us bad Christians, and deprive us of all the pleasures which our fathers enjoyed, in the hope that they would give us heaven; by these frauds subjecting us and holding us under their absolute control. And what have we to hope except to be made slaves? If we now put them all to death, we shall destroy these excrescences, and force the governor to treat us well."

The majority were carried away by his address, and rung out the war-cry of death and defiance. While still eager for blood, their chief led them to the Indian town of Tapoqui, the mission of Father Montes, on the Cano de la Leche;

tumultuously rushing in, they informed the missionary of the fate of Father Corpa, and that they sought his own life and those of all his order; and then with uplifted weapons bade him prepare to die. He reasoned and remonstrated with them, portraying the folly and wickedness of their intentions, that the vengeance of the Spaniards would surely overtake them, and implored them with tears, that for their own sakes rather than his, they would pause in their mad designs. But all in vain; they were alike insensible to his eloquence, and his tears, and pressed forward to surround him. Finding all else vain, he begged as a last favor that he should be permitted to celebrate mass before he died. In this he was probably actuated in part by the hope that their fierce hatred might be assuaged by the sight of the ceremonies of their faith, or that the delay might afford time for succor from the adjoining garrison.

The permission was given; and there for the last time the worthy Father put on his robes, which might well be termed his robes of sacrifice. The wild and savage crowd, thirsting for his blood, reclined upon the floor and looked on in sullen silence, awaiting the conclusion of the rites. The priest alone, standing before the altar, proceeded with this most sad and solemn mass, then cast his eyes to heaven and knelt in private supplication; where the next moment he fell under the blows of his cruel foes, bespattering the altar at which he ministered, with his own life's blood. His crushed remains were thrown into the fields, that they might serve for the fowls of the air or the beasts of the forest: but not one would approach it, except a dog, which, rushing forward to lay hold upon the body, fell dead upon the spot, says the ancient chronicle; and an old Christian Indian, recognizing it, gave it sepulture in the forest.

From thence the ferocious young chief of Guale led his followers against several missions, in other parts of the country, which he attacked and destroyed, together with their attendant clergy. Thus upon the soil of the ancient city was shed the blood of Christian martyrs, who were laboring with a zeal well worthy of emulation, to carry the truths of religion to the native tribes of Florida. Two hundred and sixty years have passed away since these sad scenes were enacted; but we cannot even now repress a tear of sympathy and a feeling of admiration for those self-denying missionaries of the cross, who sealed their faith with their blood, and fell victims to their energy and devotion. The spectacle of the dying priest struck down at the altar, attired in his sacred vestments, and perhaps imploring pardon upon his murderers, cannot fail to call up in the heart of the most insensible, something more than a passing emotion.

The zeal of the Franciscans was only increased by this disaster, and each succeeding year brought additions to their number. They pushed their missions into the interior of the country so rapidly that in less than two years they had established through the principal towns of the Indians no less than twenty mission houses. The presumed remains of these establishments are still occasionally to be found throughout the interior of the country.

CHAPTER XII.

SUBJECTION OF THE APALACHIAN INDIANS—CONSTRUCTION OF THE FORT, SEA WALL, &c.—1638—1700.

In the year 1638, hostilities were entered into between the Spanish settlements on the coast, and the Apalachian Indians, who occupied the country in the neighborhood of the river Suwanee. The Spaniards soon succeeded in subduing their Indian foes; and in 1640, large numbers of the Apalachian Indians were brought to St. Augustine, and in alleged punishment for their outbreak, and with a sagacious eye to the convenience of the arrangement, were forced to labor upon the public works and fortifications of the city. At this period the English settlements along the coast to the northward, had begun to be formed, much to the uneasiness and displeasure of the Spanish crown, which for a long period claimed, by virtue of exploration and occupation, as well as by the ancient papal grant of Alexander, all the eastern coast of the United States. Their missionaries had penetrated Virginia before the settlement at Jamestown: and they had built a fort in South Carolina, and kept up a garrison for some years in it. But the Spanish government had become too feeble to compete with either the English or the French on the seas; and with the loss of their celebrated Armada, perished forever their pretensions as a naval power. They were therefore forced to look to the safety of their already established settlements in Florida; and the easy capture of the fort at St. Augustine by the passing squadron of Drake, evinced the necessity of works of a much more formidable character.

It is evident that the fort, or castle as it was usually designated, had been then commenced, although its form was afterwards changed; and for sixty years subsequently, these unfortunate Apalachian Indians were compelled to labor upon the works, until in 1680, upon the recommendation of their mission Fathers, they were relieved from further compulsory labor, with the understanding that in case of necessity they would resume their labors.

In 1648, St. Augustine is described to have contained

more than three hundred householders (*vecinos*), a flourishing monastry of the order of St. Francis with fifty Franciscans, men very zealous for the conversion of the Indians, and regarded by their countrymen with the highest veneration. Besides these there were in the city alone, a vicar, a parochial curate, a superior sacristan, and a chaplain attached to the castle. The parish church was built of wood, the Bishop of Cuba, it is said, not being able to afford anything better, his whole income being but four hundred pezos per annum, which he shared with Florida; and sometimes he expended much more than his receipts.

In 1665, Captain Davis, one of the English buccaneers and freebooters (then very numerous in the West Indies), with a fleet of seven or eight vessels came on the coast from Jamaica, to intercept the Spanish plate fleet on its return from New Spain to Europe; but being disappointed in this scheme, he proceded along the coast of Florida, and came off St. Augustine, where he landed and marched directly upon the town, which he sacked and plundered, without meeting the least opposition or resistance from the Spaniards, although they had then a garrison of two hundred men in the fort, which at that time was an octagon, fortified and defended by round towers.

The fortifications, if this account be true, were probably then very incomplete; and with a vastly inferior force it is not surprising that they did not undertake what could only have been an ineffectual resistance. It does not appear that the fort was taken; and the inhabitants retired probably within its enclosure with their valuables.*

In the Spanish account of the various occurrences in this country, it is mentioned that in 1681, "the English having examined a province of Florida, distant twelve leagues from another called New Castle, where the air is pleasant, the climate mild, and the lands very fertile, called it Salvania; and that knowing these advantages, a Quaker, or Shaker (a sect barbarous impudent, and abominable), called William Penn, obtained a grant of it from Charles II., King of England, and made great efforts to colonize it." Such was the extent then claimed for the province of Florida, and such the opinion entertained of the Quakers.

In 1681, Don Juan Marquez Cabrera, applied himself at once, upon his appointment to the governorship of Florida, to finishing the castle; and collected large quantities of

---

* I do not find any account of this expedition and capture of St. Augustine in the Ensayo Cronologica

stone, lime, timber, and iron, more than sufficient subsequently to complete it. About this period, a new impulse was given to the extension of the missions for converting the Indians; and large reinforcements of the clerical force were received from Mexico, Havana, and Spain; and many of them received salaries from the crown. A considerable Indian town is spoken of at this period, as existing six hundred varas north of St. Augustine, and called Macarasi, which would correspond to the place formerly occupied by Judge Douglas, deceased, and which has long been called Macariz. Other parts of the country were known by various names. Amelia Island was the province of Guale. The southern part of the country was known as the province of Carlos. Indian river was the province of Ys. Westwardly was the province of Apalachic; while smaller divisions were designated by the names of the chiefs.

It is hardly to be doubted, that the same spirit of oppression towards the Indians, exercised in the other colonies under Spanish dominition, existed in Florida. It has been already mentioned that the Apalachians were kept at labor upon the fortifications of St. Augustine; and in 1680, the Yemasees, who had always been particularly peaceful and manageable, and whose principal town was Macarisqui, near St. Augustine, revolted at the rule exercised over them by the Spanish authorities at St. Augustine, in consequence of the execution of one of their chiefs by the order of the governor; and six years afterwards they made a general attack upon the Spaniards, drove them within the walls of the castle, and became such mortal enemies to them, that they never gave a Spaniard quarter, waylaying, and invariably massacring, any stragglers they could intercept outside of the fort.

In 1670, an English settlement was established near Port Royal, South Carolina, one hundred and five years subsequent to the settlement of St. Augustine. The Spaniards regarded it as an infringement upon their rights; and although a treaty, after this settlement, had been made between Spain and England, confirming to the latter all her settlements and islands, yet as no boundaries or limits were mentioned, their respective rights and boundaries remained a subject of dispute for seventy years.

About 1675, the Spanish authorities at St. Augustine, having intelligence from *white servants* who fled to them, of the discontented and miserable situation of the colony in Carolina, advanced with a party under arms as far as the

Island of St. Helena, to dislodge or destroy the settlers. A treacherous colonist of the name of Fitzpatrick, deserted to the Spaniards; but the governor, Sir John Yeamans, having received a reinforcement, held his ground; and a detachment of fifty volunteers under Colonel Godfrey, marched against the enemy, forcing them to retire from the Island of St. Helena, and retreat to St. Augustine.*

Ten years afterwards, three galleys sailed from St. Augustine, and attacked a Scotch and English settlement at Port Royal, which had been founded by Lord Cardross, in 1681. The settlement was weak and unprotected, and the Spaniards fell upon them, killed several, whipped many, plundered all, and broke up the colony. Flushed with success, they continued their depredations on Edisto River, burning the houses, wasting the plantations, and robbing the settlers; and finished their marauding expedition by capturing the brother of Governor Morton, and burning him alive in one of the galleys which a hurricane had driven so high upon land as to make it impossible to have it re-launched. Such at least is the English account of the matter; and they say that intestine troubles alone prevented immediate and signal retaliation by the South Carolinians.†

One Captain Don Juan de Aila went to Spain in the year 1687, in his own vessel, to procure additional forces and ammunition for the garrison at St. Augustine. He received the men and munitions desired; and as a reward for his diligence and patriotism, he also received the privilege of carrying merchandise, duty free; being also allowed to take twelve Spanish negroes for the cultivation of the fields of Florida, of whom it is said there was a great want in that province. By a mischance, he was only able to carry one negro there, with the troops and other cargo, and was received in the city with universal joy. This was the first occasion of the reception of African slaves; although as has been heretofore mentioned, it was made a part of the royal stipulation with Menendez, that he should bring over five hundred negro slaves.

Don Diego de Quiroga y Losada, the governor of Florida in 1690, finding that the sea was making dangerous encroachments upon the shores of the town, and had reached even the houses, threatening to swallow them up, and ren

---

* Carroll's S. C., Vol. 1, p. 62.

† Rivers' S. C. Hist. Coll. p. 143. Do. Appendix, 425. Carroll's Coll., 2d vol., 350.

der useless the fort which had cost so much to put in the state of completion in which it then was, called a public meeting of the chief men and citizens of the place, and proposed to them that in order to escape the danger which menaced them, and to restrain the force of the sea, they should construct a wall, which should run from the castle and cover and protect the city from all danger of the sea. The inhabitants not only approved of his proposal, but began the work with so much zeal, that the soldiers gave more than seventeen hundred dollars of their wages, although they were very much behind, not having been paid in six years; with which the governor began to make the necessary preparations, and sent forward a dispatch to the home government upon the subject.

The council of war of the Indies approved, in the following year, of the work of the sea wall, and directed the viceroy of New Spain to furnish ten thousand dollars for it, and directed that a plan and estimate of the work should be forwarded. Quiroga was succeeded in the governorship of Florida, by Don Laureano de Torres, who went forward with the work of the sea wall, and received for this purpose the means furnished by the soldiers, and one thousand dollars more, which they offered besides the two thousand dollars, and likewise six thousand dollars which had come from New Spain, remitted by the viceroy, Count de Galleo, for the purpose of building a tower, as a look-out to observe the surrounding Indian settlements. Whether this tower was erected, or where, we have no certain knowledge. The towers erected on the governor's palace and at the northeast angle of the fort, were intended as look-outs both sea and landward.

The statements made in reference to the building of this wall, from the castle as far as the city, confirm the opinion previously expressed, that the ancient and early settlement of the place was south of the public square, as the remains of the ancient sea wall extend to the basin at the Plaza. The top of this old sea wall is still visible along the centre of Bay street, where it occasionally appears above the level of the street; and its general plan and arrangement are shown on several old maps and plans of the city. Upon a plan of the city made in 1665, it is represented as terminating in a species of break-water at the public square. It is unnesessary to add that the present sea wall is a much superior structure to the old, and extends above twice the distance. Its cost is said to have been one hundred thousand dollars, and it was building from 1837 to 1843.

In the year 1700, the work on the sea wall had progressed but slowly, although the governor had employed thirty stone-cutters at a time, and had eight yoke of oxen drawing stone to the landing, and two lime-kilns all the while at work. But the money previously provided, and considerable additional funds was requisite, resembling in this respect its successor. The new governor, De Cuniga, took the matter in hand, as he had much experience in fortifications. The defenses of the fort are spoken of as being at the time too weak to resist artillery, and the sea wall as being but a slight work.

CHAPTER XIII.

ATTACK ON ST. AUGUSTINE BY GOVERNOR MOORE OF SOUTH CAROLINA—DIFFICULTIES WITH THE GEORGIANS. 1702—1732.

Hostilities had broken out between England and Spain in 1702. The English settlements in Carolina only numbered six or seven thousand inhabitants, when Governor Moore, who was an ambitious and energetic man, but with serious defects of character, led an invading force from Carolina against St. Augustine. The pretense was to retaliate for old injuries, and, by taking the initiative, to prevent an attack upon themselves. The real motive was said by Gov. Moore's opponents at home, to have been the acquisition of military reputation and private gain.

The plan of the expedition embraced a combined land and naval attack : and for this purpose six hundred provincial militia were embodied, with an equal number of Indian allies ; a portion of the militia, with the Indians, were to go inland by boats and by land, under the command of Col. Daniel, who is spoken of as a good officer, while the main body proceeded with the govenor by sea in several merchant schooners and ships which had been impressed for the service.

The Spaniards, who had received intimations of the contemplated attack, placed themselves in the best posture of defense in their power, and laid up provisions in the castle to withstand a long siege.

The forces under Col. Daniel arrived in advance of the naval fleet of the expedition, and immediately marched upon the town. The inhabitants, upon his approach, retired with their most valuable effects within the spacious walls of the castle, and Col. Daniel entered and took possession of the town, the larger part of which, it must be recollected, was at some distance from the castle.

The quaint description of these events, given by Oldmixon, is as follows :—

" Col. Rob. Daniel, a very brave man, commanded a party who were to go up the river in periagas, and come upon

Augustino on the land side, while the Governour sailed thither, and attacked it by sea. They both set out in August, 1702. Col. Daniel, in his way, took St. Johns, a small Spanish settlement; as also St. Mary's, another little village belonging to the Spaniards; after which he proceeded to Augustino, came before the town, entered and took it, Col. Moor not being yet arrived with the fleet.

"The inhabitants having notice of the approach of the English, had packed up their best effects and retired with them into the castle, which was surrounded by a very deep and broad moat.

"They had laid up provisions there for four months, and resolved to defend themselves to the last extremity. However, Col. Daniel found a considerable booty in the town. The next day the Governour came ashore, and his troops following him, they entrenched, posted their guards in the church, and blocked up the castle. The English held possession of the town a whole month; but finding they could do nothing for want of mortars and bombs, they despatched away a sloop for Jamaica; but the commander of the sloop, instead of going thither, came to Carolina out of fear of treachery. Finding others offered to go in his stead, he proceeded in the voyage himself, after he had lain some time at Charlestown.

"The Governour all this while lay before the castle of Augustino, in expectation of the return of the sloop, which hearing nothing of, he sent Col. Daniel, who was the life of the action, to Jamaica on the same errand.

"This gentleman, being hearty in the design, procured a supply of bombs, and returned towards Augustino. But in the mean time two ships appeared in the offing, which being taken to be two very large men of war, the Governour tho't fit to raise the siege and abandon his ships, with a great quantity of stores, ammunition, and provisions, to the enemy. Upon which the two men of war entered the port of Augustino, and took the Governour's ships. Some say he burnt them himself. Certain it is they were lost to the English, and that he returned to Charles-Town over land 300 miles from Augustino. The two men of war that were thought to be so large, proved to be two small frigates, one of 82, and the other of 16 guns.*

---

* There must be an error, of course, in this statement of an 82-gun ship entering St. Augustine, as the depth of water would never admit a vessel of over 300 tons: probably 82 should read 12 tons.   G. R. F.

"When Col. Daniel came back to St. Augustine, he was chased, but got away; and Col. Moor retreated with no great honor homewards. The periagas lay at St. Johns, whither the Governour retired and so to Charles-Town, having lost but two men in the whole expedition."

Arratomakaw, king of the Yamioscans, who commanded the Indians, retreated to the periagas with the rest, and there slept upon his oars with a great deal of bravery and unconcern. The governor's soldiers, taking a false alarm, and thinking the Spaniards were coming, did not like this slow pace of the Indian king in his flight, and to quicken him into it, bade him make more haste. But he replied, "No; though your governor leaves you, I will not stir till I have seen all my men before me."

The Spanish accounts say that he burned the town, and this statement is confirmed by the report made on the 18th July, 1740, by a committee of the House of Commons of the province of South Carolina, in which it is said, referring to these transactions, that Moore was obliged to retreat, *but not without* first burning the town.*

It seems that the plunder carried off by Moore's troops was considerable; as his enemies charged at the time that he sent off a sloop-load to Jamaica, and in an old colonial document of South Carolina it is represented "that the late unfortunate, ill-contrived, and worst managed expedition against St. Augustine, was principally set on foot by the said late governor and his adherents; and that if any person in the said late assembly undertook to speak against it, and to show how unfit and unable we were at that time for such an attempt, he was presently looked upon by them as an enemy and traitor to his country, and reviled and affronted in the said assembly; although the true design of the said expedition was no other than catching and making slaves of Indians for private advantage, and impoverishing the country. * * * And that the expedition was to enrich themselves will appear particularly, because whatsoever booty, as rich silks, great quantity of church plate, with a great many other costly church ornaments and utensils taken by our soldiers at St. Augustine, are now detained in the possession of the said late governor and his officers, contrary to an act of assembly made for an equal division of the same amongst the soldiers." †

---

* Carroll's Hist. Coll., vol. 2, p. 352.
† Rivers' Hist. Sketches, S. C., app. 456.

The Spanish accounts of this expedition of Moore's are very meager. They designate him as the governor of St. George, by which name they called the harbor of Charleston; and they also speak of the plunder of the town, and the burning of the greater part of the houses. Don Joseph de Curriga was the then governor of the city, and had received just previous to the English attack, reinforcements from Havana, and had repaired and strengthened the fortifications.

The retreat of the English was celebrated with great rejoicing by the Spaniards, who had been for three months shut up within the limited space of the walls of the castle: and they gladly repaired their ruined homes, and made good the ravages of the English invasion. An English account says that the two vessels which appeared off the bar and caused Moore's precipitate retreat, contained but two hundred men, and that had he awaited Colonel Daniel's return with the siege guns and ammunition, the castle would have fallen into their hands.

In the same year, the king of Spain, alarmed at the dangers which menaced his possessions in Florida, gave greater attention to the strengthening the defenses of St. Augustine, and forwarded considerable reinforcements to the garrison, as well as additional supplies of munitions.

The works were directed to be strengthened, which Governor Cuniga thought not as strong as had been represented, and that the sea wall in the process of erection was insufficient for the purpose for which it was designed.

Sixty years had elapsed since the Apalachian Indians had been conquered and compelled to labor upon the fortifications of St. Augustine; their chiefs now asked that they might be relieved from further compulsory labor; and after the usual number of references and reports and informations, through the Spanish circumlocution offices, this was graciously granted in a suspensory form, until their services should be again required.

During the year 1712, a great scarcity of provisions, caused by the failure of the usual supply vessels, reduced the inhabitants of St. Augustine to the verge of starvation; and, for two or three months, they were obliged to live upon horses, cats, dogs, and other disgusting animals. It seems strange, that after a settlement of nearly one hundred and fifty years, the Spaniards in Florida should still be dependant upon the importation of provisions for their support; and that anything like the distress indicated should prevail, with the abundant resources they had, from the fish, oysters, turtle, and clams of the sea, and the arrow-root and cabbage-tree palm of the land.

The English settlements were now extending into the interior portions of South Carolina; and the French had renewed their efforts at settlement and colonization upon the rivers discharging into the Gulf of Mexico. All three nations were competitors for the trade with the Indians, and kept up an intriguing rivalship for this trade for more than a hundred years.

There seems to have been at this period a policy pursued by the Spanish authorities in Florida, of the most reprehensible character. The strongest efforts were made to attach all the Indian tribes to the Spanish interest; and they were encouraged to carry on a system of plunder and annoyance upon the English settlements of Carolina. They particularly seized upon all the negroes they could obtain, and carried them to the governor at St. Augustine, who invariably refused to surrender them, alleging that he was acting under the instructions of his government in so doing.

In 1704, Governor Moore had made a sweeping and vigorous excursion against the Indian towns in Middle Florida, all of whom were in the Spanish interest; and had broken up and destroyed the towns and missions attached to them. In 1725, Col. Palmer determined, since no satisfaction could be obtained for the incursions of the Spanish Indians, and the loss of their slaves, to make a descent upon them; and with a party of three hundred men entered Florida, with an intention of visiting upon the province all the desolation of retributive warfare.

He went up to the very gates of St. Augustine, and compelled the inhabitants to seek protection within the castle. In his course he swept every thing before him, destroying every house, field and improvement within his reach; carrying off the live stock, and every thing else of value. The Spanish Indians who fell within his power, were slain in large numbers, and many were taken prisoners. Outside of the walls of St. Augustine, nothing was left undestroyed; and the Spanish authorities received a memorable lesson in the law of retribution.

CHAPTER XIV.

SIEGE OF ST. AUGUSTINE, BY OGLETHORPE—1732—1740

DIFFICULTIES existed for many years subsequently between the Spanish and English settlements. In 1732, Oglethorpe planted his colony in Georgia, and extended his settlements along the coast towards Florida, claiming and occupying the country up to the margin of the St. Johns, and established a post at St. George Island. This was deemed an invasion of the territory of Spain; and the post was attacked unfairly, as the English say, and some of their men murdered. Oglethorpe, upon this, acting under the instructions of the home government, commenced hostilities by arranging a joint attack of the forces of South Carolina and Georgia, with a view to the entire conquest of Florida.

The instructions of the king of England to Oglethorpe, were, that he should make a naval and land attack upon St. Augustine; "and if it shall please God to give you success, you are either to demolish the fort and bastions, or put a garrison in it, in case you shall have men enough for that purpose; which last, it is thought, will be the best way to prevent the Spaniards from endeavoring to retake and settle the said place again, at any time hereafter." *

Don Manuel Monteano was then governor of Florida, and in command of the garrison. The city and castle were previously in a poor condition to withstand an attack from a well-prepared foe; and on the 11th November, 1737, Governor Monteano writes to the governor-general of Cuba, that "the fort of this place is its only defense; it has no casemates for the shelter of the men, nor the necessary elevation to the counter-scarp, nor covert ways, nor ravelins to the curtains, nor other exterior works that could give time for a long defense; but it is thus naked outside, as it is without soul within, for there are no cannon that could be fired twenty-four hours, and though there were, artillery-men to manage them are wanting."

Under the superintendence of an able officer of engineers,

---
* State Papers of Georgia. Ga. Hist. Soc.

Don Antonio de Arredondo, the works were put in order; the ramparts were heightened and casemated; a covered way was made, by planting and embanking four thousand stakes; bomb-proof vaults were constructed, and entrenchments thrown up around the town, protected by ten salient angles, many of which are still visible. The garrison of the town was about seven hundred and forty soldiers, according to Governor Montcano's return of troops. On the 25th March, 1740, the total population of St. Augustine, of all classes, was two thousand one hundred and forty-three.

Previous to his attack upon the place, General Oglethorpe obtained the following information from prisoners whom he took at the outposts. He says: "They agree that there are fifty pieces of cannon in the castle at St. Augustine, several of which are of brass, from twelve to forty-eight pounds. It has four bastions. The walls are of stone, and casemated. The internal square is sixty yards. The ditch is forty feet wide, and twelve feet deep, six of which is sometimes filled with water. The counterscarp is faced with stone. They have lately made a covered way. The town is fortified with an entrenchment, salient angles and redoubts, which inclose about half a mile in length, and a quarter of a mile in width. The inhabitants and garrison, men, women and children, amount to above two thousand five hundred. For the garrison, the king pays eight companies, sent from Spain two years since for the invasion of Georgia; upon establishment fifty-three men each, three companies of foot and one of artillery, of the old garrison, and one troop of horse one hundred each upon establishment; of these, one hundred are at St. Marks, ten days' march from St. Augustine; upon the Gulf of Mexico, one hundred are disposed in several small forts."

Of these out-posts, there were two, one on each side of the river St. Johns—at Picolata and immediately opposite— and at Diego. The purpose of the forts at Picolata was to guard the passage of the river, and to keep open the communication with St. Marks and Pensacola; and when threatened with the invasion of Oglethorpe, messengers were dispatched to the governor of Pensacola for aid, and also to Mexico by the same route. The fort at Diego was but a small work, erected by Don Diego de Spinosa, upon his own estate; and the remains of it, with one or two cannon, are still visible. Fort Moosa was an out-post at the place now known by that name, on the North River, about two miles north of St. Augustine. A fortified line, a considerable portion of which may now be traced, extended across from the stockades on the St. Sebastian to Fort Moosa. Communication by a tide-creek existed through the marshes, between the castle at St. Augustine and Fort Moosa.

Oglethorpe first attacked the two forts at Picolata, one of which, called Fort Poppa, or St. Francis de Poppa, was a place of some strength. Its remains still exist, about one-fourth of a mile north of the termination of the Bellamy Road, its earthworks being still strongly marked.

After a slight resistance, both forts fell into his hands, much to the annoyance of Governor Monteano. Oglethorpe speaks of Fort Francis as being of much importance, "as commanding the passes from St. Augustine to Mexico, and into the country of the Creek Indians, and also being upon the ferry, where the troops which come from St. Augustine must pass." He found in it, one mortar piece, two carriages, three small guns, ammunition, one hundred and fifty shells, and fifty glass bottles full of gunpowder, with fuses—a somewhat novel missile of war.

The English general's plan of operation was, that the crews and troops upon the vessels should land, and throw up batteries upon Anastasia Island, from thence bombarding the town; while he himself designed to lead the attack on the land side. Having arrived in position, he gave the signal of attack to the fleet, by sending up a rocket; but no response came from the vessels, and he had the mortification of being obliged to withdraw his troops. The troops were unable to effect a landing from the vessels, in consequence of a number of armed Spanish galleys having been drawn up inside the bar; so that no landing could be made except under a severe fire, while the galleys were protected from an attack by the ships, in consequence of the shoal water.

He then prepared to reduce the town by a regular siege, with a strict blockade by sea. He hoped, by driving the inhabitants into the castle, so to encumber the governor with useless mouths, as to reduce him to the necessity of a surrender, to avoid starvation. The town was placed under the range of his heavy artillery and mortars, and soon became untenable, forcing the citizens generally to seek the shelter of the fort.

Col. Vanderduysen was posted at Point Quartel; and others of the troops upon Anastasia Island, and the north beach. Three batteries were erected: one on Anastasia Island, called the Poza, which consisted of four eighteen-pounders and one nine-pounder; one on the point of the wood of the island, mounting two eighteen-pounders. The remains of the Poza battery are still to be seen, almost as distinctly marked as on the day of its erection. Four mortars and forty cohorns were employed in the siege.

The siege began on the 12th June; and on the 25th June a night sortie was made from the castle against a portion of the troops under command of Col. Palmer, who were encamped at Fort Moosa, including a company of Scotch Highlanders, numbering eighty-five men, under their chief, Capt. McIntosh, all equipped in Highland dress. This attack was entirely successful, and the English sustained a severe loss, their colonel being killed, with twenty Highlanders, twenty-seven soldiers, and a number of Indians.

This affair at Fort Moosa has generally been considered as a surprise, and its disastrous results as the consequence of carelessness and disobedience of the orders of Oglethorpe. Captain McIntosh, the leader of the Highlanders, was taken prisoner, and finally transferred to Spain. From his prison at St. Sebastian, under date of 20th June, 1741, he gives the following account of the matter:—

" I listed seventy men, all in Highland dress, and marched to the siege, and was ordered to scout nigh St. Augustine and molest the enemy, while the general and the rest of his little army went to an island where we could have no succor of them. I punctually obeyed my orders, until seven hundred Spaniards sallied out from the garrison, an hour before daylight. *They did not surprise us*, for we were all under arms, ready to receive them, which we did briskly, keeping a constant firing for a quarter of an hour, when they prest on with numbers; was obliged to take our swords until the most of us were shot and cut to pieces. You are to observe we had but eighty men; and the engagement was in view of the rest of our army, but they could not come to our assistance, by being in the foresaid island, under the enemy's guns. They had twenty prisoners, a few got off, the rest killed; as we were well informed by some of themselves, they had three hundred killed on the spot,* besides several wounded. We were all stripped naked of clothes, brought to St. Augustine, where we remained three months in close confinement.†

---

* This statement is unsupported by either Spanish or English authority. The writer of the letter, through want of familiarity with their language, misunderstood his informants, in all probability, as to the extent of their loss.

† MSS. in Geo. Hist. Soc. Library.

This officer was Capt. John McIntosh; and his son, Brig. Gen. McIntosh, then a youth of fourteen, was present in the engagement, and escaped without injury. The family of the McIntoshes have always been conspicuous in the history of Georgia.

The large number of persons collected within the walls of the castle, and under the protection of its battlements, soon gave rise to serious apprehensions on the part of the besieged, of being reduced by starvation to the necessity of a speedy surrender. The batteries of Oglethorpe were planted at so great a distance that he could produce but little effect by his shot or shells upon the castle, although he rendered the city itself untenable. The heat of the season and the exposure, to which the Provincial militia were unaccustomed, soon produced considerable sickness and discouragement in the invading force, and affected Oglethorpe himself.

The Spanish governor sent most urgent messages to the governor of the island of Cuba, which were transmitted by runners along the coast, and thence by small vessels across to Havana. In one of these letters he says, "My greatest anxiety is for provisions; and if they do not come, there is no doubt of our dying by the hands of hunger." In another, he says, "I assure your Lordship, that it is impossible to express the confusion of the place; for we have no protection except the fort, and all the rest is open field. The families have abandoned their houses, and come to put themselves under the guns, which is pitiable; though nothing gives me anxiety but the want of provisions; and if your Lordship for want of competent force cannot send relief, we all must perish." *

With the exception of the Fort Moosa affair, the hostilities were confined to the exchange of shots between the castle and the batteries. Considerable discrepancy exists between the Spanish and English accounts, as to the period when the garrison was relieved: it was the communication of the fact of relief having been received, which formed the ostensible ground of abandoning the siege by Oglethorpe; but the Spanish governor asserts that these provision vessels did not arrive until the siege was raised. The real fact, I am inclined to think, is that the provision vessels arrived at Mosquito, a harbor sixty miles below, where they were to await orders from Gov. Monteano, as to the mode of getting

---

* Monteano, MSS., Archives St. Augustine.

discharged,* and that the information of their arrival, being known at St. Augustine, was communicated to the English, and thus induced their raising the siege; in fact, the hope of starving out the garrison was the only hope left to Oglethorpe; his strength was insufficient for an assault, and his means inadequate to reduce the castle, which was well manned and well provided with means of defense.

It was in truth a hopeless task, under the circumstances, for Oglethorpe to persevere; and it is no impeachment of his courage or his generalship, that he was unable to take a fortress of really very respectable strength.

The siege continued from the 13th June to the 20th July, a period of thirty-eight days. The bombardment was kept up twenty days, but owing to the lightness of the guns and the long range, but little effect was produced on the strong walls of the castle. Its spongy, infrangible walls received the balls from the batteries like a cotton bale, or sand battery, almost without making an impression; this may be seen on examination, since the marks remain to this day, as they were left at the end of the siege, one hundred and seventeen years ago.

The prosecution of the siege having become impracticable, preparations were made for retiring; and Oglethorpe, as a pardonable and characteristic protest against the assumption of his acting from any coercion, with drums beating and banners displayed, crossed over to the main land, and marched in full view of the castle, to his encampment three miles distant, situated probably at the point now known as Pass Navarro.

Great credit and respect have been deservedly awarded to Governor Monteano, for the courage, skill, and perseverance with which he sustained the siege.

It is well known that the English general had, in a few months, an ample opportunity of showing to his opponent that his skill in defending his own territory under the most disadvantageous circumstances, was equal to that of the accomplished Monteano himself. The defense of Frederica, and signal defeat of the Spanish forces at Fort Simons, will ever challenge for Oglethorpe the highest credit for the most sterling qualities of a good general and a great man.

Two years subsequently, Oglethorpe again advanced into Florida, appeared before the gates of St. Augustine, and endeavored to induce the garrison to march out to meet him; but they kept within their walls, and Oglethorpe in

---

* Monteano, MS. Letter of, 28th July, 1740.

one of his despatches says, in the irritation caused by their prudence, "that they were so meek there was no provoking them." As in this incursion he had no object in view but a devastation of the country, and harrassing the enemy, he shortly withdrew his forces.

A committee of the South Carolina House of Commons, in a report upon the Oglethorpe expedition, thus speaks of St. Augustine, evidently smarting under the disappointment of their recent defeat.

"JULY 1ST, 1741."

"St. Augustine, in the possession of the crown of Spain, is well known to be situated but little distance from hence, in latitude thirty degrees, in Florida, the next territory to us. It is maintained by his Catholic Majesty, partly to preserve his claim to Florida, and partly that it may be of service to the plate-fleets when coming through the gulf, by showing lights to them along the coast, and by being ready to give assistance when any of them are cast away thereabout. The castle, by the largest account, doth not cover more than one acre of ground, but is allowed on all hands to be a place of great strength, and hath been usually garrisoned with about three or four hundred men of the king's regular troops. The town is not very large, and but indifferently fortified. The inhabitants, many of which are mulattoes of savage dispositions, are all in the king's pay; also being registered from their birth, and a severe penalty laid on any master of a vessel that shall attempt to carry any of them off. These are formed into a militia, and have been generally computed to be near about the same number as the regular troops. Thus relying wholly on the king's pay for their subsistence, their thoughts never turned to trade or even agriculture, but depending on foreign supplies for the most common necessaries of life, they spent their time in universal, perpetual idleness. From such a state, mischievous inclinations naturally spring up in such a people; and having leisure and opportunity, ever since they had a neighbor the fruits of whose industry excited their desires and envy, they have not failed to carry those inclinations into action as often as they could, without the least regard to peace or war subsisting between the two crowns of Great Britain and Spain, or to stipulations agreed upon between the two governments."*

---

*Report upon Expedition to St. Augustine. Carroll's Coll. 2d vol., p. 354.

Among the principal grievances set forth in this report, was the carrying off and enticing and harboring their slaves, of which a number of instances are enumerated; and they attributed the negro insurrection which occurred in South Carolina, in 1739, to the connivance and agency of the Spanish authorities at St. Augustine; and they proceed in a climax of indignation to hurl their denunciation at the supposed authors of their misfortunes, in the following terms: "With indignation we looked at St. Augustine (like another Sallee!) That den of thieves and ruffians! receptacle of debtors, servants and slaves! bane of industry and society! and revolved in our minds all the injuries this province had received from thence, ever since its first settlement. That they had from first to last, in times of profoundest peace, both publickly and privately, by themselves, Indians, and Negroes, in every shape molested us, not without some instances of uncommon cruelty."*

It is very certain there was on each side, enough supposed causes of provocation to induce a far from amiable state of feeling between these neighboring colonies.

---

* Carroll's Hist. Coll. S. C. p. 359.

CHAPTER XV.

COMPLETION OF THE CASTLE—DESCRIPTIONS OF ST. AUGUSTINE A CENTURY AGO—ENGLISH OCCUPATION OF FLORIDA. 1755—1763—1783.

Don Alonzo Fernandez de Herrera was appointed governor of Florida in 1755, and completed the exterior works and finish of the fort. It is this governor who erected the tablet over its main entrance, with the Spanish coat of arms sculptured in *alto relievo*, with the following inscription beneath:—

REYNANDO EN ESPANA EL SEN^R
DON FERNANDO SEXTO Y SIENDO
GOV^{OR} Y CAP^N DE ES^A C^D S^{AN} AUG^N DE
LA FLORIDA Y SUS PROV^A EL MARISCAL
DE CAMPO D^N ALONZO FERN^{DO} HEREDA
ASI CONCLUIO ESTE CASTILLO EL AN
OD 1756 DIRIGENDO LAS OBRAS EL
CAP. INGN^{RO} DN PEDRO DE BROZAS
Y GARAY.

Don Ferdinand the Sixth, being king of Spain, and the Field Marshal, Don Alonzo Fernando Hereda, being Governor and Captain General of this place, St. Augustine, of Florida, and its province. This fort was finished in the year 1756. The works were directed by the Captain Engineer, Don Pedro de Brazos y Garay.

I am not sure but that the boastful governor might with equal propriety and truth have put a similar inscription at the city gate, claiming the town also as a finished city.

The first fort erected was called San Juan de Pinos, and probably the same name attached to the present fort at the commencement of its erection; when it acquired the name of St. Mark, I have not discovered. The Apalachian Indians were employed upon it for more than sixty years, and to their efforts are probably due the evidences of immense labor in the construction of the ditch, the ramparts and glacis, and the approaches; while the huge mass of stone contained in its solid walls, must have required the labor of hundreds of persons for many long years, in procuring and cutting the stone in the quarries on the island, transporting it to the water, and across the bay, and fashioning and raising them to their places. Besides the Indians employed, some labor was constantly bestowed by the garrison; and, for a considerable period, convicts were brought hither from Mexico to carry on the public works. During the works of extension and repair effected by Monteano, previous to the siege by Oglethorpe, he employed upon it one hundred and forty of these Mexican convicts. The southwestern bastion is said to have been completed by Monteano. The bastions bore the names respectively of St. Paul, St. Peter, St. James, &c.

The whole work remains now as it was in 1756, with the exception of the water battery, which was reconstructed by the government of the United States in 1842-3. The complement of its guns is one hundred, and its full garrison establishment requires one thousand men. It is built upon the plan of Vauban, and is considered by military men as a very creditable work; its strength and efficiency have been well tested in the old times; for it has never been taken, although twice besieged, and several times attacked. Its frowning battlements and sepulchral vaults will long stand after we and those of our day shall be numbered with that long past, of which it is itself a memorial; of its legends connected with the dark chambers and prison vaults, the chains, the instruments of torture, the skeletons walled in, its closed and hidden recesses—of Coacouchee's escape, and many another tale, there is much to say; but it is better said within its grim walls, where the eye and the imagination can go together, in weaving a web of mystery and awe over its sad associations, to the music of the grating bolt, the echoing tread, and the clanking chain.

Of the city itself, we have the following description in 1754:—

"It is built on a little bay, at the foot of a hill shaded by trees, and forms an oblong square, divided into four streets, and has two full streets, which cut each other at right angles. The houses are well built, and regular. They have only one church, which is called after the city. St. John's Fort, standing about a mile north of it, is a strong, irregular fortification, well mounted with cannon, and capable of making a long defense."

I am inclined to think that the *mile* between the fort and the city, and the *hill* at the foot of which, he says, the city was built, existed only in the focus of the writer's spectacles.

The Provinces of Florida were ceded by treaty to England in the year 1763, and the Spanish inhabitants very generally left the country, which had then been under Spanish rule for near two hundred years; and certainly in no portion of this country had less progress been made. Beyond the walls occupied by its garrison, little had been attempted or accomplished in these two hundred years. This was in part, perhaps, attributable to the circumstances of the country—the frequent hostility of the Indians, and the want of that mutual support given by neighborhoods, which in Florida are less practicable than elsewhere; but it was still more owing to the character of the Spanish inhabitants, who were more soldiers than civilians, and more townsmen than agriculturists; at all events, at the cession of Florida to Great Britain, the number of inhabitants was not over five thousand.

Of the period of the English occupation of Florida, we have very full accounts. It was a primary object with the British government, to colonize and settle it; and inducements to emigrants were strongly put forth, in various publications. The work of Roberts was the first of these, and was followed in a few years by those of Bartram, Stork, and Romans. The works of both Roberts and Stork, contain plans and minute descriptions of St. Augustine. The plan of the town in Stork, represents every building, lot, garden, and flower-bed in the place, and gives a very accurate view of its general appearance.

The descriptions vary somewhat. Roberts, who published his work the year of the cession, 1763, shows in connection with his plan of the town, an Indian village on the point south of the city, at the powder-house, and another just north of the city. The one to the north has a church. A negro fort is shown about a mile to the northward. Oglethorpe's landing place is shown on Anastasia Island, and a small fort on the main land south of the city. The depth of water on the bar is marked as being at low water, eight feet.

Roberts describes the city as "running along the shore at the foot of a pleasant hill, adorned with trees; its form is oblong, divided by four regular streets, crossing each other at right angles; down by the sea side, about three-fourths of a mile south of the town, standeth the church, and a monastery of St. Augustine. The best built part of the town is on the north side, leading to the castle, which is called St. John's Fort. It is a square building of soft stone, fortified with whole bastions, having a rampart of twenty feet high, with a parapet nine feet high, and it is casemated. The town is fortified with bastions, and with cannon. On the north and south, without the walls of the city, are the Indian towns."

The next plan we have, is in the work by Dr. Stork, the third edition of which was published in 1769. He gives a beautiful plan of the place. Shows the fort as it now exists, with its various outworks; three churches are designated, one on the public square at its southwest corner; another on St. George street, on the lot on the west side, south of Green lane, and a Dutch church near where the Roman Catholic cemetery now exists. From the size of the plan, it does not embrace the Indian village. The present United States Court-house was the governor's official residence, and is represented as having attached to it a beautiful garden. The Franciscan house or convent is shown where the barracks are now, but different in the form of the buildings. With the exception of the disappearance of a part of one street then existing, there appears very little change from the present plan of the town and buildings.

He describes the fort as being finished "according to the modern taste of military architecture," and as making a very handsome appearance, and "that it might justly be deemed the prettiest fort in the king's dominion." He omits the pleasant hill from his description, and says "the town is situated near the glacis of the fort; the streets are regularly laid out, and built narrow for the purposes of shade. It is above half a mile in length, regularly fortified with bastions, half-bastions, and a ditch; that it had also several rows of the Spanish bayonet along the ditch, which formed so close a chevaux de frize, with their pointed leaves, as to be impenetrable; the southern bastions were built of stone. In the middle of the town is a spacious square, called the parade, open towards the harbor; at the bottom of the square is the governor's house, the apartments of which are spacious and suitable; suited to the climate, with high windows, a balcony in front, and galleries on both sides; to the back of the house is joined a tower, called in America a look-out, from which there is an extensive prospect towards the sea, as well as inland. There are two churches within the walls of the town, the parish church, a plain building, and another belonging to the convent of Franciscan Friars, which is converted into barracks for the garrison. The houses are built of free-stone, commonly two stories high, two rooms upon a floor, with large windows and balconies; before the entry of most of the houses, runs a portico of stone arches. The roofs are commonly flat. The Spaniards consulted convenience more than taste in their buildings. The number of houses within the town and lines, when the Spaniards left it, was about nine hundred; many of them, especially in the suburbs, being built of wood, are now gone to decay. The inhabitants were of all colors, whites, negroes, mulattoes, Indians, &c. At the evacuation of St. Augustine, the population was five thousand seven hundred, including the garrison of two thousand five hundred men. Half a mile from the town to the west, is a line with a broad ditch and bastions, running from the St. Sebastian creek to St. Marks river. A mile further is another fortified line with some redoubts, forming a second communication between a stoccata fort upon St. Sebastian river, and Fort Moosa, upon St. Marks river.

"Within the first line near the town, was a small settlement of Germans, who had a church of their own. Upon the St. Marks river, within the second line, was also an Indian town, with a church built of freestone; what is very remarkable, it is in good taste, though built by the Indians."

The two lines of defense here spoken of, may still be traced. The nearest one is less than one-fourth of a mile from the city gate, and the other at the well-known place called the stockades, the stakes driven to form which, still distinctly mark the place; and the ditch and embankment can be traced for a considerable distance through the grounds attached to my residence.

A letter-writer, who dates at St. Augustine, May, 1774, says, "This town is now truly become a heap of ruins, a fit receptacle for the wretches of inhabitants." (Rather a dyspeptic description, in all probability.)

A bridge was built across the Sebastian river by the English, "but the great depth of the water, joined to the instability of the bottom, did not suffer it to remain long, and a ferry is now established in its room; the keeper of the ferry has fifty pounds per annum allowed him, and the inhabitants pay nothing for crossing, except after dark."

The English constructed large buildings for barracks, characterized by Romans "as such stupendous piles of buildings, which were large enough to contain five regiments, when it is a matter of great doubt whether there will ever be a necessity to keep one whole regiment here. The material for this great barracks was brought from New York, and far inferior to those found on the spot; yet the freight alone amounted to more than their value when landed. It makes us almost believe," says the elaborate Romans, "that all this show is in vain, or at most, that the English were so much in dread of musquitoes, that they thought a large army requisite to drive off these formidable foes. To be serious," says he, "this fort and barracks add not a little to the beauty of the prospect; but most men would think that the money spent on this useless parade, would have been better laid out on roads and fences through the province; or, if it must be in forts, why not at Pensacola?"

There is a manuscript work of John Gerard Williams de Brahm, existing in the library of Harvard University, which contains some particulars of interest, relative to Florida at the period of the English occupation.

He states the number of inhabitants of East Florida, which in those days meant mostly St. Augustine, from 1663 to 1771, as follows: householders, besides women, &c., two hundred and eighty-eight; imported by Mr. Turnbull from Minorca, &c., one thousand four hundred; negroes, upwards of nine hundred. Of these, white heads of families, one hundred and forty-four were married, which is just one-half; thirty-one are storekeepers and traders; three haberdashers, fifteen innkeepers, forty-five artificers and mechanics, one hundred and ten planters, four hunters, six cow-keepers, eleven overseers, twelve draftsmen in employ of government, besides mathematicians; fifty-eight had left the province; twenty-eight dead, of whom four were killed acting as constables, two hanged for pirating. Among the names of those then residing in East Florida are mentioned Sir Charles Burdett, William Drayton, Esq., planter, Chief Justice; Rev. John Forbes, parson, Judge of Admiralty and Councillor; Rev. N. Fraser, parson at Musquito; Governor James Grant, Hon. John Moultrie, planter and Lieutenant Governor; William Stork, Esq., historian; Andrew Turnbull, Esq., H. M. Counselor; Bernard Romans, draftsman, &c.; William Bartram, planter; James Moultrie, Esq.

He says, The light house on Anastasia Island had been constructed and built of mason-work by the Spaniards; and, in 1769, by order of General Haldimand, it was raised sixty feet higher in carpenter's work, had a cannon planted on the top, which is fired the very moment the flag is hoisted, for a signal to the town and pilots that a vessel is off. The light house has two flag-staffs, one to the south and one to the north; on either of which the flag is hoisted, viz., to the south if the vessel comes from thence, and the north if the vessel comes that way.

"The town is situated in a healthy zone, is surrounded with salt water marshes, not at all prejudicial to health; their evaporations are swept away in the day time by the easterly winds, and in the night season by the westerly winds trading back to the eastward. At the time when the Spaniards left the town, all the gardens were well stocked with fruit trees, viz., figs, guavas, plantain, pomegranates, lemons, limes, citrons, shadock, bergamot, China and Seville oranges, the latter full of fruit throughout the whole winter season; and the pot-herbs, though suspended in their vegetation, were seldom destroyed by cold. The town is three-quarters of a mile in length, but not quite a quarter wide; had four churches ornamently built with stone in the Spanish taste, of which one within and one without the town still exist. One is pulled down; that is the German church, but the steeple is preserved as an ornament to the town; and the other, viz., the convent church and convent in town is taken in the body of the barracks. All houses are built of masonry; their entrances are shaded by piazzas, supported by Tuscan pillars or pilasters, against the south sun. The houses have to the east windows projecting sixteen or eighteen inches into the street, very wide, and proportionally high. On the west side, their windows are commonly very small, and no opening of any kind to the north, on which side they have double walls six or eight feet asunder, forming a kind of gallery, which answers for cellars and pantries. Before most of the entrances were arbors of vines, producing plenty and very good grapes. No house has any chimney for a fire-place; the Spaniards made use of stone urns, filled them with coals left in their kitchens in the afternoon, and set them at sunset in their bed-rooms, to defend themselves against those winter seasons, which required such care. The governor's residence has both sides piazzas, viz., a double one to the south, and a single one to the north; also a Belvidere and a grand portico decorated with Doric pillars and entablatures. On the north end of the town is a casemated fort, with four bastions, a ravelin, counterscarp, and a glacis built with quarried shell-stones, and constructed according to the rudiments of Marechal de Vauban. This fort commands the road of the bay, the town, its environs, and both Tolomako stream and Mantanzas creek. The soil in the gardens and environs of the town is chiefly sandy and marshy. The Spaniards seem to have had a notion of manuring their land with shells one foot deep.

"Among the three thousand who evacuated St. Augustine, the author is credibly informed, were many Spaniards near and above the age of one hundred years, (observe;) this nation, especially natives of St. Augustine, bore the reputation of great sobriety."*

On the 3d of January, 1766, the themometer sunk to 26° with the wind from N. W. "The ground was frozen an inch thick on the banks; this was the fatal night that destroyed the lime, citron, and banana trees in St. Augustine, and many curious evergreens up the river that were twenty years old in a flourishing state."† In 1774 there was a snow storm, which extended over most of the province. The ancient inhabitants still (1836) speak of it as an extraordinary white rain. It was said to have done little damage.‡

In this connection, and as it is sometimes supposed that the climate is now colder than formerly, it may be stated that the thermometer went very low in 1799. East Florida suffered from a violent frost on the 6th April, 1828. In February, 1835, the thermometor sunk to 7° above zero, wind ftom N. W.; and the St. Johns river was frozen several rods from the shore; all kinds of fruit trees were killed to the ground, and the wild orange trees suffered as well as the cultivated.

Dr. Nicholas Turnbull, in the year 1767, associated with Sir William Duncan and other Englishmen of note, projected a colony of European emigrants, to be settled at New Smyrna. He brought from the islands of Greece, Corsica, and Minorca, some fourteen hundred persons, agreeing to convey them free of expense, find them in clothing and provisions, and, at the end of three years, to give fifty acres of land to each head of a family, and twenty-five to each child.

---

* De Brahm MS., p. 192.
† Stork, p. 11.
‡ Williams' Florida, p. 17.

After a long passage they arrived out, and formed the settlement. The principal article of cultivation produced by them was indigo, which commanded a high price, and was assisted by a bounty from the English government. After a few years, Turnbull, as is alleged, either from avarice or natural cruelty, assumed a control the most absolute over these colonists, and practiced cruelties the most painful upon them.

An insurrection took place in 1769 among them, in consequence of severe punishments, which was speedily repressed, and the leaders of it brought to trial before the English court at St. Augustine; five of the number were convicted and sentenced to death. Gov. Grant pardoned two of the five, and a third was released upon the condition of his becoming the executioner of the other two. Nine years after the commencement of their settlement, their number had become reduced from 1,400 to 600. In 1776, proceedings were instituted on their behalf by Mr. Yonge, the attorney-general of the province, which resulted in their being exonerated from their contract with Turnbull; lands were thereupon assigned them in the northren part of the city, which was principally built up by them; and their descendants, at the present day, form the larger portion of the population of that place.

Governor Grant was the first English governor, and was a gentleman of much energy; and during his term of office he projected many great and permanent improvements in the province. The public roads, known as the king's roads, from St. Augustine to New Smyrna, and from St. Augustine to Jacksonville, and thence to Coleraine, were then constructed, and remain a lasting monument of his wisdom and desire of improvement.

Gov. Tonyn succeeded Gov. Grant; and a legislative council was authorized to assemble, and the pretense and forms of a constitutional government were gone through with.

In August, 1775, a British vessel called the Betsey, Capt. Lofthouse, from London, with 111 barrels of powder, was captured off the bar of St. Augustine, by an American privateer from Charleston, very much to the disgust and annoyance of the British authorities.

At this period, St. Augustine assumed much importance as a depot and *point d'appui* for the British forces in their operations against the Southern States; and very considerabe forces were at times assembled.

In the excess of the zeal and loyalty of the garrison and inhabitants of St. Augustine, upon the receipt of the news of the American Declaration of Independence, the effigies of John Hancock and Samuel Adams were burned upon the public square, where the monument now stands.

The expedition of Gen. Prevost against Savannah was organized and embarked from St. Augustine, in 1779.

Sixty of the most distinguished citizens of Carolina were seized by the British in 1780, and transported to St. Augustine as prisoners of war and hostages, among whom were Arthur Middleton, Edward Rutledge, Gen. Gadsden, and Mr. Calhoun; all were put upon parole except Gen. Gadsden and Mr. Calhoun, who refused the indulgence, and were committed to the fort, where they remained many months close prisoners. Gen. Rutherford and Col. Isaacs, of North Carolina, were also transported hither, and committed to the fort.

An expedition was fitted out from St. Augustine in 1783, to act against New Providence, under Col. Devereux; and, with very slender means that able officer succeeded in capturing and reducing the Bahamas, which have ever since remained under English domination.

The expense of supporting the government of East Florida during the English occupation, was very considerable, amounting to the sum of £122,000. The exports of Florida, in 1778, amounted to £48,000; and in 1772, the province exported 40,000 lbs. indigo; and in 1782, 20,000 barrels of turpentine.

CHAPTER XVI.

RE-CESSION OF FLORIDA TO SPAIN—ERECTION OF THE PARISH CHURCH—CHANGE OF FLAGS. 1783—1821.

In June, 1784, in fulfillment of the treaty between England and Spain, Florida, after twenty years of British occupation, was re-ceded to the Spanish Crown, and taken possession of by Governor Zespedez.

The English residents, in general, left* the country, and went either to the Bahamas, Jamaica, or the United States. Those who went to the British islands were almost ruined: but those who settled in the States were more successful.

In April, 1793, the present Roman Catholic church was commenced, the previous church having been in another portion of the city.† It was constructed under the direction of Don Mariana de la Rocque and Don P. Berrio, government engineer-officers. The cost of the church was $16,650, of which about $6,000 was received from the proceeds of the materials and ornaments of the old churches, about $1,000 from the contributions of the inhabitants, and the remaining $10,000 furnished by the government. One of its four bells has the following inscription, showing it to be probably the oldest bell in this country, being now 185 years old.

Sancte Joseph.
Ora Pro Nobis.
D 1682.

Don Enrique White was for many years governor of Florida, and died in the city of St. Augustine. He is spoken of by those who knew him, in high terms, for his integrity

---
* Among the families remaining were the Fatios, Flemings, and a few others.

† The old parish church was on St. George street, on west side of the street.

and openness of character; and many amusing anecdotes are related connected with his eccentricities.

In 1812, the American government, being apprehensive that Great Britain designed obtaining possession of Florida, sent its troops into the province, overrunning and destroying the whole country. The manner and the pretenses under which this was done, reflect but little credit on the United States government; and the transparent sham of taking possession of the country by the patriots, supported by United States troops, was as undignified as it was futile. It is for the damages occasioned by this invasion, that the "Florida claims" for "losses" of its citizens have been presented to the government of the United States. The *principal* of the damages sustained, that is to say, the actual value of the property then destroyed, has been allowed and paid; but the interest, or damages for the detention, has been withheld upon the ground that the government does not pay interest. The treaty between the United States and Spain in reference to the cession of Florida to the United States, requires the United States to make *satisfaction* for such claims; and the payment of the bare amount of actual loss, after a detention of thirty years, is considered by the claimants an inadequate *satisfaction* of a just claim.

In the spring of 1818, General Jackson made his celebrated incursion into Florida, and by a series of energetic movements followed the Seminoles and Creeks to their fastnesses, and forever crushed the power of those formidable tribes for offensive operations.

In the latter part of 1817, a revolutionary party took possession of Amelia Island, and raised a *soi disant patriot* flag at Fernandina, supported mainly in the enterprise by adventurers from the United States; M'Gregor was assisted by officers of the United States army. An expedition was sent from St. Augustine by the Spanish governor to eject the invaders, which failed. One Aury, an English adventurer, for a time held command there; and also a Mr. Hubbard, formerly sheriff of New York, who was the civil governor, and died there. The United States troops eventually interfered; but negotiations for the cession put a stop to further hostilities.

The king of Spain, finding his possessions in Florida utterly worthless to his crown, and only an expense to sustain the garrisons, while the repeated attempts to disturb its political relations prevented any beneficial progress towards its settlement, gladly agreed, in 1819, to a transfer of Florida to the United States for five millions of dollars.

An English gentleman who visited St. Augustine in 1817, gives his impressions of the place as follows: "Emerging from the solitudes and shades of the pine forests, we espied the distant yet distinct lights of the watch towers of the fortress of St. Augustine, delightful beacons to my weary pilgrimage. The clock was striking ten as I reached the foot of the drawbridge; the sentinels were passing the *alerto*, as I demanded entrance; having answered the preliminary questions, the draw-bridge was slowly lowered. The officer of the guard, having received my name and wishes, sent a communication to the governor, who issued orders for my immediate admission. On opening the gate, the guard was ready to receive me; and a file of men, with their officer, escorted me to his Excellency, who expressed his satisfaction at my revisit to Florida. I soon retired to the luxury of repose, and the following morning was greeted as an old acquaintance by the members of this little community.

"I had arrived at a season of general relaxation, on the eve of the carnival, which is celebrated with much gayety in all Catholic countries. Masks, dominoes, harlequins, punchinellos, and a great variety of grotesqe disguises, on horseback, in cars, gigs, and on foot, paraded the streets with guitars, violins, and other instruments; and in the evenings, the houses were open to receive masks, and balls were given in every direction. I was told that in their better days, when their pay was regularly remitted from the Havana, these amusements were admirably conducted, and the rich dresses exhibited on these occasions, were not eclipsed by their more fashionable friends in Cuba; but poverty had lessened their spirit for enjoyment, as well as the means for procuring it; enough, however, remained to amuse an idle spectator, and I entered with alacrity into their diversions.

"About thirty of the hunting warriors of the Seminoles, with their squaws, had arrived, for the purpose of selling the produce of the chase, consisting of bear, deer, tiger, and other skins, bears' grease, and other trifling articles. This savage race, once the lords of the ascendant, are the most formidable border enemies of the United States. This party had arrived, after a range of six months, for the purpose of sale and barter. After trafficking for their commodities, they were seen at various parts of the town, assembled in small groups, seated upon their haunches, like monkeys, passing round their bottles of *aque dente* (the rum of Cuba), their repeated draughts upon which soon exhausted their contents; they then slept off the effects of intoxication, under the walls, exposed to the influence of the sun. Their appearance was extremely wretched; their skins of a dark, dirty, chocolate color, with long, straight, black hair, over which they had spread a quantity of bears' grease. In their ears, and the cartilages of the nose, were inserted rings of silver and brass, with pendants of various shapes; their features prominent and harsh, and their eyes had a wild and ferocious expression.

"A torn blanket, or an ill-fashioned dirty linen jacket, is the general costume of these Indians; a triangular piece of cloth passes around the loins; the women vary in their apparel by merely wearing short petticoats, the original colors of which were not distinguishable from the various incrustations of dirt. Some of the young squaws were tolerably agreeable, and if well washed and dressed would not have been uninteresting; but the elder squaws wore the air of misery and debasement.

"The garrison is composed of a detachment from the Royal regiment of Cuba, with some *black* troops; who together form a respectable force. The fort and bastions are built of the same material as the houses of the town, *coquina*. This marine substance is superior to stone, not being liable to splinter from the effects of bombardment; it receives and imbeds the shot, which adds rather than detracts from its strength and security.

"The houses and the rear of the town are intersected and covered with orange groves; their golden fruit and deep green foliage, not only render the air agreeable, but beautify the appearance of this interesting little town, in the centre of which (the square) rises a large structure dedicated to the Catholic religion. At the upper end are the remains of a very considerable house, the former residence of the governor of this settlement; but now (1817), in a state of dilapidation and decay, from age and inattention.

"At the southern extremity of the town stands a large building, formerly a monastery of Carthusian Friars, but now occupied as a barrack for the troops of the garrison. At a little distance are four stacks of chimnies, the sole remains of a beautiful range of barracks, built during the occupancy of the British, from 1763 to 1783; for three years the 29th regiment was stationed there, and in that time they did not lose a single man. The proverbial salubrity of the climate, has obtained for St. Augustine the designation of the Montpelier of North America; indeed, such is the general character of the Province of East Florida.

"The governor (Copinger), is about forty-five years of age, of active and vigorous mind, anxious to promote by every means in his power the prosperity of the province confided to his command; his urbanity and other amiable qualities render him accessible to the meanest individual, and justice is sure to follow an appeal to his decision. His military talents are well known, and appreciated by his sovereign; and he now holds, in addition to the government of East Florida, the rank of Colonel in the Royal Regiment of Cuba.

"The clergy consist of the *padre* (priest of the parish), Father Cosby, a native of Wexford, in Ireland; a Franciscan friar, the chaplain to the garrison, and an inferior or curè. The social qualities of the *padre*, and the general tolerance of his feelings, render him an acceptable visitor to all his flock. The judge, treasurer, collector, and notary, are the principal officers of the establishment, besides a number of those devoted solely to the military occupations of the garrison. The whole of this society is extremely courteous to strangers; they form one family, and those little jealousies and animosities, so disgraceful to our small English communities, do not sully their meetings of friendly chit-chat, called as in Spain, *turtulias*. The women are deservedly celebrated for their charms; their lovely black eyes have a vast deal of expression; their complexions a clear brunette; much attention is paid to the arrangement of their hair; at mass they are always well dressed in black silk *basquinas* (petticoats), with the little *mantilla* (black lace veil) over their heads; the men in their military costumes; good order and temperance are their characteristic virtues; but the vice of gambling too often profanes their social haunts, from which even the fair sex are not excluded. Two days following our arrival, a ball was given by some of the inhabitants, to which I was invited. The elder couples opened it with minuets, succeeded by the younger couples displaying their handsome light figures in Spanish dances."*

The old inhabitants still speak in terms of fond regret of the place when embowered in its orange groves, and the pleasantness of its old customs and usages. Dancing formed one of their most common amusements, as it does now. The posey dance, now become obsolete, was then of almost daily occurrence, and was introduced in the following manner: The females of the family erect in a room of

---

* Voyage to Spanish Main. London, 1819. Page 116, *et seq.*

their house a neat little arbor, dressed with pots and garlands of flowers, and lit up brightly with candles. This is understood by the gentleman as an invitation to drop in and admire the beauty of their decorations. In the mean time, the lady who has prepared it, selects a partner from among her visitors, and in token of her preference, honors him with a bouquet of flowers. The gentleman who receives the bouquet becomes then, for the nonce, king of the ball, and leads out the fair donor as queen of the dance; the others take partners, and the ball is thus inaugurated, and may continue several successive evenings. Should the lady's choice fall upon an unwilling swain, which seldom happened, he could be excused by assuming the expenses of the entertainment. These assemblies were always informal, and frequented by all classes, all meeting on a level; but were conducted with the utmost politeness and decorum, for which the Spanish character is so distinguished.

The carnival amusements are still kept up to some extent, but with little of the taste and wit which formerly characterized them, and without which they degenerate into mere buffoonery.

The graceful Spanish dance, so well suited in its slow and regular movements to the inhabitants of a warm climate, has always retained the preference with the natives of the place, who dance it with that native grace and elegance of movement which seems easy and natural for every one, but is seldom equaled by the Anglo-Saxon.

CHAPTER XVII.

TRANSFER OF FLORIDA TO THE UNITED STATES—AMERICAN OCCUPATION—ANCIENT BUILDINGS, Etc.

On the 10th day of July, in the year 1821, the standard of Spain, which had been raised two hundred and fifty-six years before over St. Augustine, was finally lowered forever from the walls over which it had so long fluttered, and the stars and stripes of the youngest of nations rose where, sooner or later, the hand of destiny would assuredly have placed them.

It was intended that the change of flags should have taken place on the 4th of July; owing to a detention, this this was frustrated; but the inhabitants celebrated the 4th with a handsome public ball at the governor's house.

The Spanish garrison, and officers connected with it, returned to Cuba, and some of the Spanish families; but the larger portion of the inhabitants remained. A considerable influx of inhabitants from the adjoining States took place, and the town speedily assumed a somewhat American character. The proportion of American population since the change of flags, has been about one-third. Most of the native inhabitants converse with equal fluency in either language.

In the year 1823, the legislative council of Florida held its second session in the government house at St. Augustine. Governor W. P. Duval was the first governor after the organization of the territory. The Ralph Ringwood Sketches of Irving have given a wide celebrity to the character of our worthy and original first governor, now recently deceased.

During the month of February, 1835, East Florida was visited by a frost much more severe than any before experienced. A severe northwest wind blew ten days in succession, but more violently for about three days. During this period, the mercury sunk to seven degrees above zero. The St. Johns river was frozen several rods from the shore. All kinds of fruit trees were killed to the ground; many of them never started again, even from the roots. The wild groves suffered equally with those cultivated. The orange had become the staple of Florida commerce; several millions were exported from the St. Johns and St. Augustine during the two previous years. Numerous groves had just been planted out, and extensive nurseries could hardly supply the demand for young trees. Some of the groves had, during the previous autumn, brought to their owners, one, two, and three thousand dollars; and the increasing demand for this fruit, opened in prospect mines of wealth to the inhabitants.

"Then came a frost, a withering frost."

Some of the orange groves in East Florida were estimated at from five to ten thousand dollars, and even more. They were at once rendered valueless. The larger part of the population at St. Augustine had been accustomed to depend on the produce of their little groves of eight or ten trees, to purchase their coffee, sugar, and other necessaries from the stores; they were left without resource.

"The town of St. Augustine, that heretofore appeared like a rustic village, their white houses peeping from among the clustered boughs and golden fruit of their favorite tree, beneath whose shade the foreign invalid cooled his fevered limbs, and imbibed health from the fragrant air,—how was she fallen! Dry, unsightly poles, with ragged bark, stick up around her dwellings; and where the mocking-bird once delighted to build her nest, and tune her lovely songs, owls hoot at night, and sterile winds whistle through the leafless branches. Never was a place rendered more desolate."*

The groves were at once replanted, and soon bid fair to yield most abundantly; when, in 1842, an insect was introduced into the country, called the *orange coccus*, which spread over the whole country with wonderful rapidity, and almost totally destroyed every tree it fastened upon. Of late, the ravages of this insect seem less destructive, and the groves have begun to resume their bearing; these add to the beauty of the residences at St. Augustine, with their glossy, deep-green leaves, and golden fruit; and hopes of an entire restoration are now confidently entertained.

In December, 1835, the war with the Seminole Indians broke out; and for some years St. Augustine was full of the pomp and circumstance of war. It was dangerous to venture beyond the gates; and many sad scenes of Indian massacre took place in the neighborhood of the city. Dur-

---

* Williams' Florida, pp. 18, *et seq.*

ing this period, great apparent prosperity prevailed; property was valuable, rents were high; speculators projected one city on the north of the town, and another on the west; a canal to the St. Johns, and also a railroad to Picolata; and great hopes of future prosperity were entertained. With the cessation of the war, the importance of St. Augustine diminished; younger communities took the lead of it, aided by superior advantages of location, and greater enterprise, and St. Augustine has subsided into the pleasant, quiet, *dolce far niente* of to-day, living upon its old memories, contented, peaceful, and agreeable, and likely to remain without much change for the future.

Of the public buildings, it may be remarked that the extensive British barracks were destroyed by fire in 1792; and that the Franciscan Convent was occupied as it had been before, as barracks for the troops not in garrison in the fort. The appearance of these buildings has been much changed by the extensive repairs and alterations made by the United States government. It had formerly a large circular look-out upon the top, from which a beautiful view of the surrounding country was obtained. Its walls are probably the oldest foundations in the city.

The present United States Court-house, now occupied by many public offices, was the residence of the Spanish governors. It has been rebuilt by the United States; and its former quaint and interesting appearance has been lost, in removing its look-out tower, and balconies, and the handsome gateway, mentioned by De Brahm, which is said to have been a fine specimen of Doric architecture.*

Trinity Episcopal Church was commenced in 1827, and consecrated in 1833, by Bishop Bowen, of South Carolina. The Presbyterian Church was built about 1830, and the Methodist chapel about 1846.

The venerable-looking building on the bay, at the corner of Green lane and Bay street, is considered the oldest building in the place, and has evidently been a fine building in its day. It was the residence of the attorney-general, in English times.

The monument on the public square was erected in 1812–13, upon the information of the adoption of the Spanish constitution, as a memorial of that event, in pursuance of a royal order to that effect, directed to the public authorities of all the provincial towns. Geronimo Alvarez was

---

* It is said to have been taken down by the contractor, to form the foundation of his kitchen.

the Alcalde under whose direction it was erected. The plan of it was made by Sr. Hernandez, the father of the late General Hernandez A short time after it was put up, the Spanish constitution having had a downfall, orders were issued by the government that all the monuments erected to the constitution throughout its dominions, should be demolished. The citizens of St. Augustine were unwilling to see their monument torn down; and with the passive acquiescence of the governor, the marble tablets inscribed PLAZA DE LA CONSTITUCION being removed, the monument itself was allowed to stand; and thus it remains to this day, the only monument in existence to commemorate the farce of the constitution of 1812. In 1818, the tablets were restored without objection.

The bridge and causeway are the work of the government of the United States. The present sea-wall was built between 1835 and 1842, by the United States, at an expense of one hundred thousand dollars.

CHAPTER XVIII.

PRESENT APPEARANCE OF ST. AUGUSTINE, AS GIVEN BY THE AUTHOR OF THANATOPSIS—ITS CLIMATE AND SALUBRITY.

St. Augustine has now attained, for this side of the Atlantic, a period of most respectable antiquity. In a country like America, where States are ushered into existence in the full development of maturity, where large cities rise like magic from the rude forest, where the "oldest inhabitant" recollects the cutting down of the lofty elms which shadowed the wigwam of the red man, perchance on some spot now in the heart of a great city; an antiquity of three centuries would be esteemed as almost reaching back (compared with modern growth) to the days of the Pharaohs.

The larger number of early settlements were unsuitably located, and were forced to be abandoned on account of their unhealthiness; but the Spanish settlement at St. Augustine has remained for near three hundred years where it was originally planted; and the health of its inhabitants has, for this long period, given it a deserved reputation for salubrity and exemption from disease, attributable to locality or extraneous influences or causes.

The great age attained by its inhabitants was remarked by De Brahm; the number and healthfulness of the children that throng its streets, attract now, as they did then, the attention of strangers. This salubrity is easily accounted for, by the almost insular position of the city, upon a narrow neck of land nearly surrounded by salt water; the main shore, a high and healthy pine forest and sandy plains, so near the ocean as to be fanned by its constant breezes, and within the sound of its echoing waves; a situation combining more local advantages for salubrity could hardly be imagined. While it will never probably increase to any great extent in population, it will hardly be likely to decrease. Its health, easy means of support, unambitious class of inhabitants, with their strong attachments and family and local ties, will contribute to maintain St. Augustine as the time-honored ancient city, with its permanent population, and its visitors for health, for centuries perhaps yet to come.

I cannot perhaps better conclude these historic notices than by giving the impressions of the author of Thanatopsis,* one whose poetic fame will endure as long as American literature exists. Writing from St. Augustine in April, 1843, he says:

" At length we emerged upon a shrubby plain, and finally came in sight of this oldest city of the United States, seated among its trees on a sandy swell of land, where it has stood for three hundred years. I was struck with its ancient and homely aspect, even at a distance, and could not help likening it to pictures which I had seen of Dutch towns, though it wanted a wind-mill or two to make the resemblance perfect. We drove into a green square, in the midst of which was a monument erected to commemorate the Spanish constitution of 1812, and thence through the narrow streets of the city to our hotel.

"I have called the streets narrow. In few places are they wide enough to allow two carriages to pass abreast. I was told that they were not originally intended for carriages; and that in the time when the town belonged to Spain, many of them were floored with an artificial stone, composed of shells and mortar, which in this climate takes and keeps the hardness of rock; and that no other vehicle than a hand-barrow was allowed to pass over them. In some places you see remnants of this ancient pavement; but for the most part it has been ground into dust under the wheels of the carts and carriages introduced by the new inhabitants. The old houses, built of a kind of stone which is seemingly a pure concretion of small shells, overhang the streets with their wooden balconies; and the gardens between the houses are fenced on the side of the street with high walls of stone. Peeping over these walls you see branches of the pomegranate, and of the orange-tree now fragrant with flowers, and rising yet higher, the leaning boughs of the fig with its broad luxuriant leaves. Occasionally you pass the ruins of houses—walls of stone with arches and stair-cases of the same material, which once belonged to stately dwellings. You meet in the streets with men of swarthy complexions and foreign physiognomy, and you hear them speaking to each other in a strange language. You are told that these are the remains of those who inhabited the country under the Spanish dominion, and that the dialect you have heard is that of the island of Minorca.

---

* Bryant.

"'Twelve years ago,' said an acquaintance of mine. 'when I first visited St. Augustine, it was a fine old Spanish town. A large proportion of the houses which you now see roofed like barns, where then flat-roofed; they were all of shell rock, and these modern wooden buildings were then not erected. That old fort which they are now repairing, to fit it for receiving a garrison, was a sort of ruin, for the outworks had partly fallen, and it stood unoccupied by the military, a venerable monument of the Spanish dominion. But the orange-groves were the wealth and ornament of St. Augustine, and their produce maintained the inhabitants in comfort. Orange-trees of the size and height of the pear-tree, often rising higher than the roofs of the houses, embowered the town in perpetual verdure. They stood so close in the groves that they excluded the sun; and the atmosphere was at all times aromatic with their leaves and fruit, and in spring the fragrance of the flowers was almost oppressive.'

"The old fort of St. Mark, now called Fort Marion—a foolish change of name—is a noble work, frowning over the Mantanzas, which flows between St. Augustine and the island of Anastasia; and it is worth making a long journey to see. No record remains of its original construction; but it is supposed to have been erected about a hundred and fifty years since,* and the shell rock of which it is built is dark with time. We saw where it had been struck with cannon balls, which, instead of splitting the rock, became imbedded and clogged among the loosened fragments of shell. This rock is therefore one of the best materials for fortification in the world. We were taken into the ancient prisons of the fort-dungeons, one of which was dimly lighted by a grated window, and another entirely without light; and by the flame of a torch we were shown the half obliterated inscriptions scrawled on the walls long ago by prisoners. But in another corner of the fort, we were taken to look at the secret cells, which were discovered a few years since in consequence of the sinking of the earth over a narrow apartment between them. These cells are deep under ground, vaulted over-head, and without windows. In one of them a wooden machine was found, which some supposed might have been a rack, and in the other a quantity of human bones. The doors of these cells had been walled up and concealed with stucco, before the fort passed into the hands of the Americans.

* It is much more ancient.

"You cannot be in St. Augustine a day without hearing some of its inhabitants speak of its agreeable climate. During the sixteen days of my residence here, the weather has certainly been as delightful as I could imagine. We have the temperature of early June as June is known in New York. The mornings are sometimes a little sultry; but after two or three hours a fresh breeze comes in from the sea sweeping through the broad piazzas, and breathing in at the windows. At this season it comes laden with the fragrance of the flowers of the Pride of India, and sometimes of the orange tree, and sometimes brings the scent of roses, now in bloom. The nights are gratefully cool; and I have been told by a person who has lived here many years, that there are very few nights in summer when you can sleep without a blanket.

"An acquaintance of mine, an invalid, who has tried various climates, and has kept up a kind of running fight with death for many years, retreating from country to country as he pursued, declares to me that the winter climate of St. Augustine is to be preferred to that of any part of Europe, even that of Sicily, and that it is better than the climate of the West Indies. He finds it genial and equable, at the same time that it is not enfeebling. The summer heats are prevented from being intense by the sea-breeze, of which I have spoken. I have looked over the work of Dr. Forry on the climate of the United States, and have been surprised to see the uniformity of climate which he ascribes to Key West. As appears by the observations he has collected, the seasons at that place glide into each other by the softest gradations; and the heat never, even in midsummer, reaches that extreme which is felt in the higher latitudes of the American continent. The climate of Florida is, in fact, an insular climate: the Atlantic on the east, and the Gulf of Mexico on the west, temper the airs that blow over it, making them cooler in summer and warmer in winter. I do not wonder, therefore, that it is so much the resort of invalids; it would be more so if the softness of its atmosphere, and the beauty and serenity of its seasons were generally known. Nor should it be supposed that accommodations for persons in delicate health are wanting; they are, in fact, becoming better with every year, as the demand for them increases. Among the acquaintances whom I have made here, I remember many who having come hither for the benefit of their health, are detained for life by the amenity of the climate. 'It seems to me,' said an intelligent gentleman of this class, the other

8

day, 'as if I could not exist out of Florida. When I go to the north, I feel most sensibly the severe extremes of the weather; the climate of Charleston itself appears harsh to me.'

"The negroes of St. Augustine are a good-looking specimen of the race, and have the appearance of being very well treated. You rarely see a negro in ragged clothing; and the colored children, though slaves, are often dressed with great neatness. In the colored people whom I saw in the Catholic church, I remarked a more agreeable, open, and gentle physiogomy than I have been accustomed to see in that class.

"Some old customs which the Minorcans brought with them from their native country, are still kept up. On the evening before Easter Sunday, about eleven o'clock, I heard the sound of a serenade in the streets. Going out, I found a party of young men with instruments of music, grouped about the window of one of the dwellings, singing a hymn in honor of the Virgin,* in the Mahonese dialect. They began, as I was told, with tapping on the shutter. An answering knock within had told them that their visit was welcome, and they immediately began the serenade. If no reply had been heard, they would have passed on to another dwelling. I give the hymn as it was kindly taken down for me in writing, by a native of St Augustine. I presume this is the first time that it has been put in print; but I fear the copy has several corruptions, occasioned by the unskillfulness of the copyist. The letter *e*, which I have put in italics, represents the guttural French *e*, or, perhaps, more nearly the sound of the *u* in the word but. The *sh* of our language is represented by *sc* followed by an *i* or an *e*; the *g*, both hard and soft, has the same sound as in our language.

"' Disciar*e*m lu dol
Cantar*e*m aub' alagria
Y n'ar*e*m a da
Las pascuas a Maria
O Maria!
"' Sant Grabiel,
Qui portaba la ambasciado
Des nostro rey del cel,
Estaran vos prenada
Ya omitiada
Tu o vais aqui surventa
Fia del Dieu contenta
Para fe lo que el vol
Disciar*e*m lu dol, &c.

---

* This song is usually called the *Fromajordis*.

"'Y a milla nit
Pariguero vos regina
A un Dieu infinit,
Dintra una establina.
Y a milla dia,
Que los angles von cantant
Pau y abondant
De la gloria de Dieu sol
   Disciarem lu dol, &c.

"'Y a Libalam,
Alla la terra santa
Nus nat Jesus
Aub' alagria tanta
Infant petit
Que tot lu mon salvaria
Y ningu y bastaria
Nu mes un Dieu tot sul
   Disciarem lu dol, &c.

"'Cuant de Orion lus
Tres reys la stralla veran
Dieu omnipotent
Adora lo vingaran
Un present inferan
De mil encens y or
A lu beneit seno
Que conesce cual se vol
   Disciarem lu dol, &c.

"'Tot fu gayant
Para cumple la prumas
Y lu Esperit sant
De un angel fau granas
Gran foc ences,
Que crama lu curagia
Dieu nos da lenguagia
Para fe lo que Dieu vol
   Disciarem lu dol, &c.

"'Cuant trespasa
De quest mon nostra Senora
Al cel s' empugia
Sun fil la matescia ora
O! Emperadora
Que del cel san eligida
Lu rosa florida
Me resplenden que un sol
   Disciarem lu dol, &c.

"'Y el tercer giorn
Que Jesus resunta
Dieu y Aboroma
Que la mort triumfa
De alli se balla
Para perldra Lucife
An tot a sen penda
Que de nostro ser el sol
   Disciarem lu dol, &c.'

"After this hymn, the following stanzas, soliciting the customary gift of cakes or eggs, are sung:—

"'Ce set que vam cantant,
Regina celestial!
Damos pan y alagria
Y bonas festas tingan
Y vos da sus bonas festas
Danos dines de sus nous
Sempre tarem lus neans Uestas
Para recibi un grapat de nos,
Y el giorn de pascua florida
Alagramos y giuntament
As qui es mort par dar nos vida
Y via glorosiamente.
A questa casa esta empedrada
Bien halla que la empedro;
San amo de aquesta casa
Baldria duna un do
Formagiado o empanada
Cucutta a flao;
Cual se val casa rue grada,
Sol que no rue digas que no.'

"The shutters are then opened by the people within, and a supply of cheese, cakes or other pastry, or eggs, is dropped into a bag carried by one of the party; who acknowledge the gift in the following lines, and then depart:—

"'Aquesta casa reta empedrada
Empedrada de cuatro vens;
San amo de aquesta casa
Es omo de compliment.'

"If nothing is given, the last line reads thus:—

"'No es homo de compliment.'"

CHAPTER XIX.

ST. AUGUSTINE IN ITS OLD AGE.—1565–1868.

THREE hundred and three years have now passed over the walls of this venerable city. Ten generations of men and women have passed away since this ancient city had an existence and a name. One can look back to 1565 and picture to the mind the galleons of Spain anchored off its harbor; see the gallant Adelantado Menendez, clad in mail, preceded by the standards of Spain, and followed by his men at arms, his bowmen and his cavaliers, taking possession of the country in the name of his sovereign. The waves roll in upon the same shores now as they did then; the green, grassy marshes and oyster-clad banks present to our eyes the same appearance as they did to theirs; the white sandy beach which received the impress of the iron-clad heel of the cavalier, now yields to the pressure of your foot; the rustling pines along the shore cast their pleasant shadows over you as they did over them, and perchance the same eager thoughts of gain pervade your breast as you pass beneath them, as filled the hearts and souls of those who long ago came seeking gold and wealth unmeasured upon those shores.

Three hundred years ago, and St. Augustine stood the solitary settlement of the white race north of the Gulf of Mexico in all that great expanse which now boasts of its thirty-four States, its three hundred cities, and its thirty millions of people.

Then the Province of Florida extended northward to the pole, and westward to the Pacific. At a later period, after the voyages of the French and English, its boundaries were limited to the shores of the Chesapeake and the Mississippi river, and were subsequently gradually contracted to their present limits, so that Florida once represented upon the maps all of the United States.

The life of St. Augustine runs parallel with that of Spain. For a long period Spain was at the head of European monarchies; its rulers held sway over more vast possessions than had ever belonged to any single crown since the days of the Cæsars; wealth flowed into its coffers from the New World in boundless profusion, and corruption, venality and effeminacy followed in its train. The whole continent of America was claimed as its dominion. Its fleets anchored upon every shore for conquest or exploration, and its banners were unfurled by its generals, and the cross was planted by its priests, upon every headland. From all this grandeur and eminence the Spanish monarchy has been cast down. Driven from land to land, it has receded from the main land of America, and has exchanged its dominion over a continent to the islands of the sea, which it holds with a precarious grasp, and it now remains in a dry old age a fourth-rate power where once it stood foremost. The first planted of all the cities of the United States, St. Augustine, now ranks among the least.

Ten years have been added to the longevity of the ancient city since the first publication of this work. Ten years do not make their mark upon the aged man as they do upon the youth launching forth into manhood, or as they do upon him who in the full measure of his matured strength is battling with life. On the nation at large, these ten years have left almost ineffaceable scars and bruises; ten years, the most important, the weightiest and the gravest of any since the throes of the great revolution which gave birth to the nation. This long sad period has left no mark upon its walls—grey and mouldy with the weight of years, and have scarcely added a tinge the more of age and sorrow—and yet the inner life of the old city has sustained a great shock. The system of servitude, which has now been swept away, was the sole dependence of many aged persons, of many poor widows and orphan children.

Servants in St. Agustine were treated with paternal kindness; they had grown up in the family of the indulgent master, had been his play-mate in infancy, and rendered willing service. They had their holidays and their balls, and were ever found in the background at all festive gatherings, enjoying, upon a privileged footing, the pleasures of the hour, looking on and commenting with pride upon the graceful movements in the dance of their young mistresses, and anon whirling each other around to the music, in the corridors, with the unrestrained exuberance of their simple and unalloyed happiness. All this has passed away, their homes are broken up, the poor widow and the orphan children have been brought to want, the sound of music and dancing no longer resound in the old streets, the privileged house-maid and man-servant no longer do their easy tasks with cheerful song and merry laugh.

The naval forces of the United States took possession of St. Augustine in 1862. Batteries had been mounted at the fort, and a small garrison of Confederate troops were in military occupation of the place, but too few in numbers to offer any resistance, and the city was surrendered by the civil authorities upon the demand of Captain Dupont. The 4th New Hampshire regiment first garrisoned the city. The old fort was brushed up and repaired, the earth-works strengthened, and barracks built on the platform. Occasionally reconnoitering parties of Confederates approached the town, and on one occasion a festive party of officers, who had gone out to Mr. Solanas, near Picolata, to attend a dance, were captured, with their music and ambulance, by Captain Dickinson, celebrated for many daring exploits. It was even believed that this daring partisan had ridden through the city at night in the guise of a Federal cavalry officer. On another occasion, the commanding officer of the garrison at St. Augustine was captured on the road from Jacksonville by a Confederate picket.

The inhabitants, isolated from all means of obtaining supplies from without the lines, were reduced to great straits. The only condition upon which they were allowed to purchase, was the acceptance of an oath of loyalty. Sympathizing strongly with the South, they were placed in an unfortunate position, and many doubtless suffered greatly. At one period, those of the citizens who had relatives in the Confederate service were ordered to leave the city. Then ensued a scene which beggars description. Men, women and children were huddled on board a vessel, and, homeless and helpless, were carried along the coast and disembarked, shelterless, on the banks of the Nassau river, to make their way to food and shelter as best they could—hardships which hardly seemed called for by any military necessity. Many of the young men of the city went into the Confederate service and served through the war with distinction, but many fell victims on the battle-field, in the hospitals, or from exposure to the rigorous climate of Virginia and Tennessee, to which they were unaccustomed.

To these misfortunes succeeded to all, sales and forcible deprivation of property, under the most rigorous construction of most rigorous laws—the unsettling of titles and the loss of mean have combined to lessen the ability of the people to do more than try to live, without much effort to improve their homes and the appearance of the city.

Some changes have taken place in the suburbs of the city. Macariz, the site of the old Indian town, belonging to the late Judge Douglas, with its beautiful groves of forest trees, has been utterly destroyed; and a once pleasant cottage home, near the stockades, dear to the writer, cared for and embellished with many things pleasant to the eye, fragrant with the ever blooming roses and honeysuckles, has, under the rude hand of war, been utterly destroyed, with its library, its furniture, and all its pleasant surroundings.

But while man's work has been to destroy, Nature has done much within these few years to restore one of its former sources of prosperity, the cultivation of the orange, which, having been at one period almost utterly destroyed by the cold, and then by the cocens insect, is now fast regaining its pristine vigor and productiveness, and promises in a few years to furnish to the city more permanent and abundant sources of prosperity than it has ever had.

With the infusion of Northern energy and capital, much could be done to further the prosperity of the old city, by building up first-class hotels and boarding-houses for visitors during the winter, by rebuilding the Picolata railway, thus facilitating access to the city, and thus a means of support could be given to its inhabitants.

I am sure that no one will feel otherwise than that its old age shall be tranquil and serene, and that its name may ever be associated with pleasant memories.

University of the South,
SEWANEE, TENN.

JUNIOR DEPARTMENT.
GEN'L. I. GORGAS, ...*Head Master.*

☞Situated on the Plateau of the Cumberland Mountains, in the Southern portion of Middle Tennessee, a location of unrivalled salubrity; temperate climate, and accessible by Rail-road communication.

Expenses of Board and Tuition very low, and vacation in the Winter season.

For information, apply to
G. R. FAIRBANKS, Gen'l Treasurer,
UNIVERSITY PLACE, TENNESSEE.

ST. MARY'S HALL, FOR GIRLS,
BURLINGTON COLLEGE,
(Preparatory Department,) for Boys,

THE BISHOP OF NEW-JERSEY, PRESIDENT.

Terms, per School Year,..*$450.*
☞ *First-Class Education, and no Extra Charges.* ☜
BURLINGTON, N. J.

UNIVERSITY OF VIRGINIA.

THIS INSTITUTION has a continuous Session of Nine Months, commencing annually on the 1st day of October, and ending on the Thursday before the 4th of July ensuing.

The organization of the Institution is very complete, embracing extensive and thorough Courses of Instruction in Literature and Science, and in the Professions of Law, Medicine and Engineering.

☞For details, estimated expenses, &c., send for Catalogue to WM. WERTENBAKER, Sec., or **S. MAUPIN,**
CHAIRMAN OF THE FACULTY.
P. O.—"UNIVERSITY OF VIRGINIA."

[From IRVING'S "CONQUEST OF FLORIDA," just published (Dec., 1868,) by PUTNAM & SON, New York.]

STORY OF JUAN ORTIZ.

Shortly after Pamphilo de Narvaez had left the village of Hirrihigua, on his disastrous march into the interior, a small vessel of his fleet, which was in quest of him, put into the bay of Espiritu Santo. Anchoring before the town, they

WASHINGTON UNIVERSITY.

Medical Department.

BALTIMORE, MD.

FACULTY:

REV. THOMAS E. BOND, M. D., President.
G. C. M. ROBERTS, M. D., LL. D., Emeritus Professor of Obstetrics and Diseases of Women and Children.
CHARLES W. CHANCELLOR, M. D., Professor of Descriptive and Surgical Anatomy.
J. P. LOGAN, M. D., Professor of the Principles and Practice of Medicine.
HARVEY L. BYRD, M. D., Professor of Obstetrics.
MARTIN P. SCOTT, M. D., Professor of the Diseases of Women & Children.
EDWARD WARREN, M. D., Professor of the Principles & Practice of Surgery.
JOHN F. MONMONIER, M. D., Professor of Physiology and General Pathology.
J. J. MOORMAN, M. D., Professor of Medical Jurisprudence and Hygiene.
FRANCIS T. MILES, M. D., Professor of Microscopic Anatomy and Practical Physiology.
JOSEPH E. CLAGETT, M. D., Professor of Materia Medica and Therapeutics.
CLARENCE MORFIT, M. D., Professor of Medical Chemistry and Pharmacy.
JOHN N. MONMONIER, M. D., Demonstrator of Anatomy.

The next regular Session of Washington University will begin on **Thursday, the first day of October,** and terminate on the 22d day of Feb'y, '69.

One Beneficiary Student from each Congressional District of the late slaveholding States, is annually received in this Institution—precedence being given to wounded and disabled soldiers.

In addition to a Daily Clinic of the most satisfactory character, this Institution has attached to it a Hospital of its own, in which every possible facility is afforded for acquiring a Practical Knowledge of Medicine and Surgery.

By a recent contract with the proper authorities, the Seaman's Hospital of the port of Baltimore has been placed exclusively under the control of the Faculty of Washington University.

Anatomical Material is abundant.

A Prize of One Hundred Dollars will be given for the best Thesis presented by a candidate for graduation.

FEES:—Matriculation, $5; Dissection, $10; Professors', $120; Graduation, $20; Beneficiary, $35, for each Session.

For additional information, address the subscriber, care of Post-office box 1,267, Baltimore, Md.

JOSEPH P. LOGAN, M. D., Dean of the Faculty.

---

saw a few Indians, who made signs for them to land, pointing to a letter in the end of a cleft reed, stuck in the ground. The Spaniards supposed, and probably with justice, that it was a letter of instruction left by Narvaez, giving information of his movements and destination. They made signs for the Indians to bring it to them. The latter, however, refused, but getting into a canoe came on board, where four of them offered to remain as hostages for such Spaniards as chose to

FLORIDA LANDS FOR SALE.

SEVERAL VALUABLE TRACTS of Land on the St. Johns river, suitable for ORANGE GROVES: and several thousand acres of valuable PLANTING and TIMBER LANDS, in St. Johns, Duval, Alachua, Putnam, Marion and Valusia counties. ☞ Will be sold in lots to suit purchasers, and upon a long credit. Apply to

J. M. FAIRBANS,
JACKSONVILLE, FLORIDA.

J. P. SANDERSON,
ATTORNEY AT LAW,
JACKSONVILLE, FLA.

FLEMING & DANIEL,
ATTORNEYS AT LAW,
JACKSONVILLE, FLA.

JAMES M. BAKER,
ATTORNEY AT LAW,
JACKSONVILLE, FLA.

B. B. ANDREWS,
ATTORNEY AT LAW,
JACKSONVILLE, FLA.

WILKINSON CALL,
ATTORNEY AT LAW,
JACKSONVILLE, FLA.

---

go on shore for the letter. Upon this, four Spaniards stepped into the canoe and were swiftly conveyed to the shore. The moment they landed, a multitude of savages rushed out of the village and surrounded them, and, at the same time, the hostages on board plunged into the sea and swam to shore. The crew of the vessel, seeing the number of the enemy, and dreading some further mishap, made sail with all haste, abandoning their luckless comrades to their fate.

DE WITT C. DAWKINS,
ATTORNEY AT LAW,
JACKSONVILLE, FLA.

W. M. IVES,
ATTORNEY AT LAW,
LAKE CITY, FLA.

J. J. FINLAY,
ATTORNEY AT LAW,
LAKE CITY, FLA.

LAND AGENCY.

LANDS BOUGHT AND SOLD,

And attention given to the Collection of Rents, and the Management, Purchase and Sale of

REAL ESTATE, OF EVERY DESCRIPTION,

☞ FOR ABSENT PARTIES, AND OTHERS, **ON REASONABLE TERMS.**

C. L. ROBINSON,
REAL-ESTATE AGENT,
Jacksonville, Fla.

The captives were conveyed with savage triumph into the village of Hirrihigua; for the whole had been a stratagem of the cacique, to get some of the white men into his power, upon whom he might wreak his vengeance. He placed his prisoners under a strong guard, until a day of religious festival. They were then stripped naked, led out into the public square of the village, and turned loose, one at a time, to be shot at with arrows. To prolong their misery and the enjoyment of their tormentors, but one Indian was allowed to shoot at a time. In this way the first three were sacrificed, and the cacique took a vindictive pleasure in beholding them, running in their agony from corner to corner, vainly seeking an asylum in every nook, until after repeated wounds they were shot to death.

M. A. DZIALYNSKI,

WHOLESALE AND RETAIL DEALER IN

Dry Goods, Clothing,

Hats, Boots and Shoes, Yankee Notions,

And GROCERIES,

Reed's Building, Bay Street,

JACKSONVILLE, Fla.

Orders from the Country promptly attended to.

C. SLAGER,

WHOLESALE AND RETAIL DEALER IN

Dry Goods, Clothing,

Shoes, Boots, Hardware, Groceries,

AND

All other Merchandize usually kept for Country Merchants and Farmers,

JACKSONVILLE, Florida.

Juan Ortiz, a youth, scarce eighteen years of age, of a noble family of Seville, was the fourth victim. As they were leading him forth, his extreme youth touched with compassion the hearts of the wife and daughters of the cacique, who interceded in his favor.

The cacique listened to their importunities, and granted for the present the life of Ortiz;—but a wretched life did he lead. From morning until evening he was employed in bringing wood and water, and was allowed but little sleep and scanty food. Not a day passed that he was not beaten. On festivals he was an object of barbarous amusement to the cacique, who would oblige him to run, from sunrise to sunset, in the public square of the village, where his companions had met their untimely end; Indians being stationed with bows and arrows, to shoot him should he halt one moment. When the day was spent, the unfortunate youth lay stretched on the hard floor of the hut, more dead than alive. At such times the wife and daughters of the cacique would come to him privately with food and clothing, and by their kind treatment his life was preserved.

TAYLOR HOUSE,
JACKSONVILLE, FLA.

Always Re-fitted for the Winter Travel.

---o---

Is situated on a retired portion of Bay Street, commanding a view of the St. Johns river, and in proximity to the landing of the Charleston Steamers. ☞ Every attention paid to visitors.

J. W. HAWKINS & CO., Proprietors.

ST. JOHN'S HOUSE,
FORSYTH ST., (near Pine,)......JACKSONVILLE, Fla.

---o---

Special Attention to Persons Arriving or Leaving by the Early Train or Boats.

☞ THIS HOUSE, entirely new, pleasantly situated, and completely fitted up, is now open for the accommodation of Travelers and Boarders.— Grateful for the liberal patronage always shown me, I respectfully solicit the continued favors of my friends at my new location, where every convenience will be offered for their pleasure and comfort.

Mrs. E. HUDNALL, Proprietress.

PRICE HOUSE,
Forsyth St., near the Depot, - - JACKSONVILLE, Fla.

---o---

S. S. ALDERMAN & CO., PROPRIETORS,
(FORMERLY OF MARIANNA, FLA.)

☞ THE BEST attention given to guests, and good accommodations, in every respect, provided.

At length the cacique, determining to put an end to his victim's existence, ordered that he should be bound down upon a wooden frame, in the form of a huge gridiron, placed in the public square, over a bed of live coals, and roasted alive.

The cries and shrieks of the poor youth reached his female protectors, and their entreaties were once more successful with the cacique. They unbound Ortiz, dragged him from the fire, and took him to their dwelling, where they bathed him with the juice of herbs, and tended him with assiduous care. After many days he recovered from his wounds, though marked with many a scar.

CATHAY HOUSE,
LAKE CITY, FLA.

Long established, & in proximity to R. R. Depot.

A. S. BARNES & CO.,
PUBLISHERS OF THE
National Series of School Books,
AND WHOLESALE
BOOKSELLERS AND STATIONERS,
111 and 113 William St., Cor. John,
NEW YORK.
Catalogue sent to Teachers, on application.

FRUITLAND NURSERIES, Augusta, Ga.
P. J. BERCKMANS, Proprietor.

Fruit Trees, Grape Vines,
PLANTS AND FLOWERING SHRUBS,
In Very Large and Varied Quantities,
Adapted to the Latitude of the Gulf and other Southern States.
☞ DESCRIPTIVE CATALOGUES, FREE, ON APPLICATION.
ROBT. C. LOWRY, Agent,.................Jacksonville, Fla.

His employment was now to guard the cemetery of the village. This was in a lonely field in the bosom of a forest. The bodies of the dead were deposited in wooden boxes, covered with boards, without any fastening except a stone or a log of wood laid upon the top; so that the bodies were often carried away by wild beasts.

In this cemetery was Ortiz stationed, with a bow and arrows, to watch day and night, and was told that should a single body be carried away, he would be burnt alive. He returned thanks to God for having freed him from the dreadful presence of the cacique, hoping to lead a better life with the dead than he had done with the living.

While watching thus one long wearisome night, sleep overpowered him towards morning. He was awakened by the falling lid of one of the chests, and, running to it, found it empty. It had contained the body of an infant recently deceased, the child of an Indian of great note.

J. M. FAIRBANKS,
BAY STREET, - - JACKSONVILLE, FLA.,

Commission Merchant,

AND DEALER IN

HAY, CORN, OATS, BRAN, PROVISIONS, FLOUR, PORK, BACON, LARD, BUTTER, &c.

Lime, Cement, Hair, Brick, Manipulated Manures,
GUANOS,
GROCERIES.
ADVANCES ON CONSIGNMENTS.

JOHN CLARK,

Forwarding and Commission Merchant,

AND WHOLESALE AND RETAIL DEALER IN

Groceries, Provisions, Hay, Grain,
LIQUORS, SEGARS, &c., &c.

———o———

Agent for the Steamers DARLINGTON and HATTIE.

JACKSONVILLE, FLA.

Ortiz doubted not some animal had dragged it away, and immediately set out in pursuit. After wandering for some time, he heard, a short distance within the woods, a noise like that of a dog gnawing bones. Warily drawing near to the spot, he dimly perceived an animal among the bushes, and invoking succor from on high, let fly an arrow at it. The thick and tangled underwood prevented him from seeing the effect of his shot, but as the animal did not stir, he flattered himself that it had been fatal; with this hope he waited until the day dawned, when he beheld his victim, a huge animal of the panther kind, lying dead, the arrow having passed through his entrails and cleft his heart.

Gathering together the mangled remains of the infant, and replacing them in the coffin, Ortiz dragged his victim in triumph to the village, with the arrow still in his body. The exploit gained him credit with the old hunters, and for some time softened even the ferocity of the cacique. The resentment of the latter, however, for the wrongs he had suffered from white men, was too bitter to be appeased. Some time after, his eldest daughter came to Ortiz, and warned him that her father had determined to sacrifice him at the next festival, which was just at hand, and that the influence of her mother, her sisters, and herself would no longer avail him. She wished him, therefore, to take refuge with a neighboring

The Spaniards in Florida:

BEING

Fairbanks' History of St. Augustine,

—*REVISED*,—

WITH ADDITIONS BY THE AUTHOR.

—o—

POCKET MAP OF THE STATE, Price $1.25,

AND

OTHER WORKS ON FLORIDA,

FOR SALE BY **C. DREW,**

Jacksonville.

H. ROBINSON,

Corner Ocean and Forsyth Sts., (adjoining Post-office,)

Jacksonville, Fla.

C. PARKHURST.   A. B. HUSSEY.

C. PARKHURST & CO.,

WHOLESALE AND RETAIL DEALERS IN

CORN, FLOUR, DRY GOODS, GROCERIES,

Hardware, Woodware, Furniture, &c.,

Ocean Street, near Bay, - - - JACKSONVILLE, Fla.

---

cacique named Mucozo, who loved her, and sought her in marriage, and who, for her sake, would befriend him. "This very night at midnight," said the kindhearted maiden, "at the northren extremity of the village you will find a trusty friend who will guide you to a bridge, about two leagues hence; on arriving there, you must send him back, that he may reach home before the morning dawn, to avoid suspicion—for well he knows that this bold act, in daring to assist you, may bring down destruction upon us both. Six leagues further on, you will come to the village of Mucozo—tell him that I have sent you, and expect him to befriend you in your extremity—I know he will do it—go, and may your God protect you!" Ortiz threw himself at the feet of his generous protectress, and

T. HARTRIDGE,

Bay Street, - - - - *Jacksonville, Fla.,*

GENERAL DEALER IN

DRY GOODS, GROCERIES, PROVISIONS,
CORN, &c., Wholesale & Retail.

—o—

Commission Consignments entrusted to him, carefully attended to.

FRANK SMITH & BRO.,
Wholesale Dealers in
GROCERIES & PROVISIONS
NO. 1 REQUA'S BLOCK,
JACKSONVILLE, FLA.

FURNITURE HOUSE,
Near the R. R. Depot,
JACKSONVILLE, FLA.

Large Supplies constantly kept on hand, and Orders promptly filled.

M. W. DREW,
Proprietor of the ICE DEPOT,
JACKSONVILLE, Fla.

---

poured out his acknowledgements for the kindness she had always shown him. The Indian guide was at the place appointed, and they left the village without alarming the warlike savages. When they came to the bridge, Ortiz sent back the guide, in obedience to the injunction of his mistress, and, continuing his flight, found himself, by break of day, on the banks of a small stream near the village of Mucozo.

Looking cautiously around, he espied two Indians fishing. As he was unacquainted with their language, and could not explain the cause of his coming, he was in dread lest they should take him for an enemy and kill him. He, therefore, ran to the place where they had deposited their weapons and seized upon them. The savages fled to the village without heeding his assurances of friendly intention. The inhabitants sallied out with bows and arrows, as though they would attack him. Ortiz fixed an arrow in his bow, but cried out at the same moment, that he came not as an enemy but as an ambassador from a female cacique to their chief. Fortunately one present understood him, and interpreted his words. On this the Indians unbent their bows, and returning with him to

BETTELINI & TOGNI,

JACKSONVILLE, FLA.,

DEALERS IN

Groceries, Provisions and Liquors.

IMPORT, DIRECT FROM FRANCE,

Champagne & Claret Wines, Cognac Brandy,

AND OTHER FRENCH GOODS.

AGENTS FOR HAVRE LINE OF PACKETS.

GEORGE A. PECK,

DEALER IN

Fine Watches, Jewelry, Silver and Plated Ware,

Also,

WOSTENHOLM'S AMERICAN CUTLERY, TOYS, &c., &c.

Ocean Street, adjoining Express Office, - - JACKSONVILLE, FLA.

THE

INTERNATION'L OCEAN TELEGRAPH
COMPANY.

WIRES extending from LAKE CITY, Fla., to HAVANA, Cuba, connecting with all Telegraph Lines in the United States, and with the Atlantic cable to Europe. *⁎* Office in Jacksonville, corner Bay and Pine streets.

W. H. HEISS, *Gen. Supt.*   WILLIAM F. SMITH, *Prest.*

---

their village, presented him to Mucozo. The latter, a youthful chieftain, of a graceful form and handsome countenance, received Ortiz kindly for the sake of her who had sent him; but, on further acquaintance, became attached to him for his own merits, treating him with the affection of a brother.

Hirrihigua soon heard where the fugitive had taken refuge, and demanded several times that he should be delivered up; Mucozo as often declined; considering himself bound by the laws of honor and hospitality to protect him. Hirrihigua

RAIL-ROAD COMMUNICATION WITH FLORIDA.

FROM SAVANNAH:

(At which point the R. R. and Steamship Lines from the North converge.)

PASSENGERS TAKE THE

Atlantic & Gulf R. R.,

WHICH INTERSECTS THE

PENSACOLA & GEORGIA ROAD,

(WHICH RUNS EAST AND WEST THROUGH FLORIDA,)

At LIVE OAK, a point mid-way between Tallahasse and Jacksonville,

FROM WHENCE THEY CAN TAKE EITHER DIRECTION.

TWO Trains are run DAILY between Savannah and Jacksonville, and ONE between Savannah and Tallahasse.

TIME, from Savannah to Jacksonville, by Express, 12 hours, *and Without Change of Cars.*

From JACKSONVILLE, Steamboats run on the St. John's River, in connection with the Road.

☞ THROUGH TICKETS can be procured in New York and other principal cities North, for TALLAHASSE, JACKSONVILLE, and all points on the St. John's, and to ST. AUGUSTINE.

The accommodations on the Roads are first class, with superior Sleeping Cars, and all other modern comforts.

R. WALKER,
General Supt. P. & G. R. R., Tallahasse.

H. S. HAINES,
General Supt. A. & G. R. R., Savannah.

C. D. OWENS,
General Business Agt. A. & G. R. R.,
No. 40 Broadway, New York.

---

then employed as mediator another cacique, a brother-in-law of Mucozo, by the name of Urribarracuxi, who went in person to demand Ortiz. The generous Mucozo, however, refused to deliver up to a cruel enemy, the poor fugitive who

BROCK'S LINE ON THE ST. JOHNS.

THE STEAMERS
DARLINGTON and HATTIE,
FORM THE LINE
Between JACKSONVILLE and ENTERPRISE, Florida,

Making at least SEMI-WEEKLY TRIPS during the Winter, and adapting their Schedule to the demands of Travel and Trade on the River:

—TOUCHING AT—

*Mandarin,**	*Hargrove's Landing,*
*Hibernia,**	*Horse Landing,*
Magnolia,	*Welaka,**
*Green-Cove Spring,**	*Salt Lake,**
*Hogarth's Wharf,**	*Georgetown,*
*Picolata,**	*Valusia,**
Tocoi,	*Hawkinsville,**
*Federal Point,**	*Cabbage Bluff,*
Orange Mills,	*Starke's Landing,*
*Dancy's Wharf,**	*Blue Spring,**
Whetstone's "	*Emanuel Landing,*
Russell's "	*Mellonville*, and*
*Palatka,**	*Enterprise*—*

(Where visitors are entertained at the BROCK HOUSE,)

And leaving Mails at such of those places as are marked with a *—affording ample opportunities to Strangers and others to visit the various localities on the **Beautiful St. John's**, and connecting with the Rail-road lines to and from Savannah.

THIS IS THE OLD-ESTABLISHED LOCAL LINE OF THE WHOLE RIVER ROUTE.

☞ For detailed information, as to Schedules of Time and Rates, apply to

JOHN CLARK, Agent,
Dock, foot of Ocean St., JACKSONVILLE, FLA.

---

had come recommended to his protection, and treated the very request as a stain upon his honor. The two caciques continued their importunities, but the high-minded savage remained faithful to his guest, though in maintaining inviolate the sacred rites of hospitality, he lost the friendship of his brother-in-law, and forfeited the hand of her he tenderly loved, the beautiful daughter of Hirrihigua.

At this juncture tidings reached Mucozo of the arrival of De Soto and his troops at the village of Hirrihigua, and that it was their intention to conquer the country. Alarmed at this intelligence, he addressed himself to Ortiz. "You all know," said he, "what I have done for you; that I have sheltered you when friendless, and have chosen rather to fall into disgrace with my relations and neighbors, than to deliver you into the hands of your enemies. This I did without thought or hope of reward, but the time has come when you can repay me for my friendship. Go to the chieftain of this army of white men—represent to him the asylum I have extended to you, and which, in like case, I would have afforded to any of your countrymen—entreat him, in return, not to lay waste my territory, and assure him that I and mine are ready to devote ourselves to his service.

Ortiz gladly departed on the mission, accompanied by fifty chosen warriors. It happened that about the same time Baltazar de Gallegos had been dispatched, as has been already mentioned, on his embassy to Mucozo.

As Ortiz and his Indian escort, therefore, were on their way to the village of Hirrihigua, they came in sight of Baltazar, and his band of lancers, glistening at a distance, in the midst of a verdant plain, skirted by a wood.

The Indians would have concealed themselves in the forest, until the Christians could be informed that they were friends; but Ortiz slighted their advice, insisting that his countrymen would at once recognize him; not reflecting that in appearance he was in nowise different from his savage companions, being like them almost naked, his body browned by exposure to the sun, his arms painted, a quiver at his back, a bow and arrow in his hand, and his head adorned with feathers.

No sooner did the Spaniards descry the savages, than they came down upon them at full gallop, heedless of the voice of their captain; for they were newly raised soldiers, full of spirit, and eager for a brush with the natives.

The Indians fled terrified to the wood. One, however, was overtaken and slain. Juan Ortiz was assaulted by Alvaro Nieto, one of the stoutest and boldest troopers in the army. Ortiz parried the thrust of his lance with his bow, running at the same time, and leaping from side to side with great agility to avoid the horse, crying out lustily Xivilla, Xivilla—meaning Seville, Seville; and making the sign of the cross with his arm and bow, to signify that he was a Christian.

Alvaro Nieto hearing him cry out Xivilla, demanded of him whether he was Juan Ortiz. On his replying in the affirmative, he seized him by the arm, lifted him upon the croup of his saddle, and scoured away to present him to Baltazar de Gallegos. The captain received him with great joy, and ordered his troopers to be recalled, who were beating up the woods and hunting the poor Indians like so many deer.

Ortiz himself went into the forrest and called to the Indians, to come out and fear nothing. Many, however, fled back to their village, to acquaint Mucozo with what had happened. Others joined Ortiz in small parties, upbraiding him with his rashness, but when they found one of their people wounded, they were so exasperated, that they would have laid violent hands upon him had not the Spaniards been present.

They were at length pacified. The soldiers bound up the wounds of the Indian, and placed him upon a horse. The troopers, having taken up all the Indians behind them, galloped away for the encampment of the governor. Previously to setting off, however, Ortiz dispatched an Indian to Mucozo, with a true account of the late events, lest that cacique should be irritated by the alarming statement brought by the fugitives.

The night was already far advanced when Baltazar de Gallegos and his band reached the camp. When the governor heard the tramp of their horse, he feared some mischance had befallen them, as he had not looked for them before the expiration of three days. His apprehensions were soon turned to rejoicing. He praised Gallegos and his men for the skill and success of their expedition, and received Ortiz as his own son, sympathizing with his past sufferings, and presenting him with a suit of clothes, arms, and a good horse. The Indians he treated with kindness, and ordered the wounded savage to be carefully attended. He then dispatched two of the natives to Mucozo, thanking him for his past kindness to Ortiz, accepting his proffers of friendship, and inviting him to the camp. Not an eye was closed this night, but one and all joined in the revelry which welcomed the liberation of poor Ortiz.

www.ingramcontent.com/pod-product-compliance
Lightning Source LLC
Chambersburg PA
CBHW030401170426
43202CB00010B/1449